DISTORTION

the DISTORTION

2000 Years of Misrepresenting the Relationship Between Jesus the Messiah and the Jewish People

DR. JOHN FISCHER AND DR. PATRICE FISCHER

Lederer Books
a division of
Messianic Jewish Publishers

About the cover:
The original painting, *This Was Not My Teaching*, hangs in the library of Messianic Jewish Publishers. After the unspeakable massacres in Ukraine during World War I, the Jewish artist, William Wachtel was compelled to express on canvas, the torment of the persecuted Jews, and Yeshua's identity with his own people.

09 08 07 06 05 04   6 5 4 3 2 1
ISBN 1-880226-25-1

Library of Congress Control Number: 2004106102
Printed in the United States of America

Lederer Books
a division of
Messianic Jewish Publishers
6204 Park Heights Ave.
Baltimore, Maryland 21215
(410) 358-6471

Distributed by
Messianic Jewish Resources International
Order line: (800) 410-7367
E-mail: lederer@messianicjewish.net
Website: www.messianicjewish.net

This book is dedicated to our parents, George and Marianne Fischer. They personally suffered the consequences of this distortion, survived the horrors and lived to tell the story, served as wonderful role models for us all, and continue to fight the distortion as they enlighten others. It is also dedicated to our children, Eve and Seth, who carry on the struggle and continue the story.

Contents

Introduction

In its March 19, 2004 edition, the *St. Petersburg Times* reported the following story. It seems that a married couple in Statesboro, Georgia, got into an argument after watching Mel Gibson's movie, *The Passion of the Christ*. When they left the theater, they were locked in vigorous debate. Then, after they got home, the argument turned violent. The two were charged with simple battery after they called the police on each other. According to the police report, the wife suffered injuries on her face and arm, while her husband had a stab wound on his hand, the result of a pair of scissors; his shirt had been ripped off. He had also punched a hole in their wall. As the wife said, "It was the dumbest thing we've ever done" ("'Passion' Stirs Couple to Battle").

Not all responses to the movie have been that passionate. However, the film has been controversial, raising the emotional level of interfaith discussions. In the process, recently formed inter-religious friendships have become strained, and old wounds among Jews and Christians have been reopened. Others have been left simply shaking their heads in amazement and confusion.

One recently married interfaith couple experienced some of these emotions first-hand, after seeing the film together. The Jewish wife was very deeply disturbed by the movie's presentation of the events, and its treatment of the Jews who were part of it, even though she could not quite put her finger on what bothered her. The Christian husband was greatly moved by the film, and could not understand his wife's concern. They simply could not appreciate each other's perspectives. Their situation illustrates some of the broader, more substantial issues that the movie has brought to the forefront once again.

How can a story that purports to be the greatest demonstration of God's compassion for humankind, the most stirring example of sacrificial love, become the source of such anguish and pain? And, how could this story, so Jewish at its core, have become an instrument of hatred—as it indeed has—over centuries of human history?

But this is not just an ancient story; it is a modern story as well. On April 5, 2004, the Associated Press reported on the response to the showing of *The Passion* in Cairo, Egypt. A 21-year-old Muslim woman from Jordan came out of the theater in tears. She told the reporter the movie "unmasked the Jews' lies, and I hope that everybody, everywhere, turns against the Jews" (Abou El-Magd).

As odd as it might sound, for the past 2000 years, the truth about the *real* relationship between Jesus the Messiah and the Jewish people has in fact been distorted. This distortion has led to all sorts of tragedies and travesties. This book was written to explain how it happened, using Gibson's film as the most recent example. It then offers some encouraging thoughts and suggestions.

We want to establish the credibility of the Gospels as originally written so people will know that these documents *actually* can be trusted. Chapter 1 answers the question, "Are the Gospels Reliable?"

Chapter 2, "Are the Gospels Anti-Semitic?" addresses one of the assumptions that is often heard. In reality, when reading many versions of the Newer Testament, one might get the impression that the gospel writers, themselves Jews, were somehow anti-Jewish. Yet, that just doesn't make any sense. This fallacy has painfully caused death and destruction to many Jewish people. This chapter shows that the Gospels are *not* anti-Semitic.

Although a sensitive question, "Has the Church Been Anti-Semitic?" needs to be answered if this book is to honestly trace the impact of the last 2000 years of the distortion. It's not that all Christians have deliberately wanted to harm Jews, it's just that we need to present the background for some awful—and often violent—acts against the people of the Messiah. Chapter 3 addresses this issue.

Using the preceding chapters as background, Chapter 4, "A Battle of Religious World Views," shows why a movie such as *The Passion of the Christ* has been so controversial in the Jewish community. Because of the immense popularity of this film, we have chosen it as an example of how centuries of misrepresentation have impacted the culture of our times. The disparity between Jewish and Christian responses to this movie demonstrates the depth of the divide that has developed because of the misrepresentations discussed in this book.

Because Gibson is a "Traditional Catholic," it is important to be aware of the influence his brand of Catholicism had on his understanding of the Newer Testament. In addition to the writings of two nuns and their "visions," the interpretations of the Passion Plays of the Middle Ages significantly affected Mr. Gibson's filmmaking decisions. This is why we have included Chapter 5, "A Modern Script for the Passion Story."

Given that the distortion is nearly 2000 years old, it was almost inevitable that Gibson, especially having the additional influence of his particular religious perspective, would make certain potentially damaging decisions. Chapter 6, "Cinematic Choices That Could Lead to Anti-Semitic Conclusions" offers several surprising examples of the results of these decisions.

Having established that misrepresentations of the gospel have existed for two millennia, Chapter 7 sets the record straight. This chapter explains how the death of Yeshua (Jesus) was actually part of God's master plan, put in motion from the beginning of humanity—a plan that began with God's people, Israel, and then expanded to the rest of the world.

Chapter 8 shows that God's plan, the promise he made to the people of Israel and brought to completion in the atoning death of Yeshua, rooted itself deeply first among his own people. And so, the chapter answers the question, "Have the Jewish People Responded to God's Plan?"

Chapter 9, "Does It Matter?" shows that even though God does have a master plan, the fact that some people haven't followed it has cost his Jewish people much. The fact is, the distortion of the plan has led to awful horror for the Jews ands significant loss to Christians.

Our final chapter, Chapter 10, offers ways to help end the distortion.

Note: Throughout this book, we have chosen to use the terms "Older" and "Newer" when referring to the "Old" and "New" Testaments. What is called the "Old" Testament isn't "old" in the sense that it is obsolete or that the study of it provides neither blessing nor instruction. It is "old" only in that it is chronologically "older" than the "newer" part of the Bible. It is still relevant and offers as much today as it did in Yeshua's day, 2000 years ago, before the distortion began. Rav Shaul (Rabbi Saul, the apostle Paul) wrote of it even before the "Newer" Testament was codified:

> All Scripture is God-breathed and is valuable for teaching truth, convicting of sin, correcting faults and training in right living; thus anyone who belongs to God may be fully equipped for every good work. (2 Tim. 3:16–17)

✡   ✡   ✡

Chapter 1

Are the Gospels Reliable?

Articles or books on the Gospels sometimes include statements such as the following:

> Scholars have argued that the gospel writers, writing many decades after the events they are describing, have tailored the details of Jesus' life to fit their own circumstances or theological agenda, so then the actual facts of his life and the details of his teachings, cannot be accurately known. The story then is really a second-century reflection of a first-century world. The Bible may *say* Yeshua walked on water or healed the sick, but he probably didn't.

How reasonable is this approach? Rabbi Berel Wein reflected on this issue.

> I have always found it difficult to understand how people, millennia after the fact, are able to interpret and reach conclusions about the ancients, conclusions that were not evident at that time to contemporaries who knew them and also escaped the attention of scholars who pored over and continually commented on the Bible and its heroes over the past many centuries. To me, it smacks of arrogance. (31)

While the rabbi's comments are very much to the point, this remains an important subject. Therefore, it needs to be dealt with in some detail. The discussion can be broken down into two parts.

Are the Gospels Later Documents, Written in the Second Century Long After the Events Took Place?

This perspective is often assumed in articles and frequently taught in universities. In other words, the Gospels are thought to be legends or inventions of second-century Christians. As it turns out, this imaginative reconstruction of the origins of the Gospels runs into several obstacles.

While there are numerous later manuscript copies of the Newer Testament, some are, in fact, quite early. The renowned papyrologist Carsten Peter Thiede closely examined several early manuscript fragments of the Gospels to determine their date of composition (*Eyewitness to Jesus*). Using paleographic considerations such as writing style and document format, he discovered that the Magdalen Papyrus (a fragment of Matthew) probably dates to about the year 70 C.E. He also noted that a typical Jewish shorthand convention in referring to God's sacred name was used by the copyist in referring to Yeshua as "Lord." This would be a rather striking indication of the manuscript's Jewish origins and of its earliness, and so helps confirm Thiede's assessment of the date of the manuscript. Jewish features of Christian beliefs quickly evaporated in the very early centuries. He also examined fragments of manuscripts of Luke and Mark. The Luke fragment was found in a Paris library and appears to be written between 63 and 67 C.E. The Mark fragment, 7Q5, was one of the Dead Sea scroll fragments found at the Qumran community. It can be quite accurately dated to 68 C.E.

In addition to Thiede's work and analysis, there is a fragmentary papyrus of John's gospel, the John Rylands manuscript. This text dates to about 110 C.E. Then, there are the numerous quotations of the Newer Testament by the early church leaders, called the Church Fathers. With the exception of a small handful of verses, the entire Newer Testament is quoted by these leaders by about 250 C.E., some 36,000 plus quotations in all. Much of this quoting comes from Clement of Rome before the year 100 C.E. What this all means is that if copies of the Gospels exist from as early as 63–110 C.E., the original documents must have been written considerably earlier than those who hold to a later writing imagine.

In ancient times, the process of writing, circulating, deteriorating, and copying of documents was a complex and extended process. Once an important document had been written, if it was broadly significant enough, it was then circulated widely among those groups to whom it was relevant. Examples of this process are mentioned in the Newer Testament itself. In Colossians 4:16 the rabbi, Rav Shaul, instructs his students in Colosse to pass his letter to them along to his students in Laodicea, and to get his letter from his Laodicean students and read that themselves. Revelation 2 and 3 contains indications that this document was intended to be read and circulated along the entire trade route from Ephesus to Laodicea. During this process of circulation, the documents eventually began to deteriorate. The deterioration of a significant document then launched its copying. Now, the copying of a document was a rather lengthy and costly procedure in and of itself. Everything was carefully copied by hand by specially trained copyists called scribes. Then, the copies entered the circulation process. Given the long span of time that was involved in the circulation, deterioration, copying, and recirculation of ancient documents, copy dates of 63–110 C.E. yield composition dates for the Gospels which are rather early.

Appropriately, the former Oxford scholar John Wenham argues in his book *Redating Matthew, Mark and Luke* that these three Gospels were written prior to 55 C.E. He came to this conclusion independent of, and prior to, Thiede's work. He derived his assessment from a close textual, intertextual, and contextual examination of the Gospels themselves. The Cambridge University scholar, J.A.T. Robinson, similarly argued for an early date for the entire Newer Testament in *Redating the New Testament*. His analysis led him to a date before 70 C.E. for the composition of all these books. He also developed evidence for John being the earliest gospel to be written (*The Priority of John*). It should be noted that Robinson's entire scholarly work on the Bible has moved in decidedly nonconservative directions both theologically and historically. Hence, his early dating of the gospel texts is especially significant. Some of the issues that both Wenham and Robinson discuss are the glaring absence of references or allusions to important episodes in the early life of Yeshua's community of followers. The destruction of the Temple; the deaths of James, Peter, and Rav Shaul; and the persecution under Nero were all highly significant events to this emerging Messianic Jewish movement. Yet, no mention is made of them.

The work of Thiede, and the analysis of Robinson, Wenham, and others are further corroborated from another source. William F. Albright was the foremost archaeologist of the Near East during the first two-thirds of the twentieth century. From his studies he concluded: "In my opinion, every book of the New Testament was written by a baptized Jew between the forties and the eighties of the first century A.D." (Albright, *Christianity Today* 18). Elsewhere, he stated: "We can already say emphatically that there is no longer any solid basis for dating any book of the New Testament after about 80 A.D." (Albright, *Recent Discoveries in Bible Lands* 136). Coming as he does from an entirely different field of scholarship, Albright's evaluation is even stronger additional reinforcement of the early date of composition for the Gospels.

Now, for a very important pertinent consideration, the ramifications of the Jewish nature of the gospel records. The fact that there is a clear Jewish thrust to, and Jewish structure underlying, the Gospels, helps make the case for an early writing of these documents. Numerous scholars have noted this fact. (Bowman, Carrington, Drury, Fischer, Goulder, Guilding, Roth, et al.) Matthew paints Yeshua against the backdrop of Moses and Daniel. Mark has him as a rabbi and as a prophet following in the footsteps of Elijah and Elisha. Luke presents him as the priest-king who reflects not only David, but Joseph as well. John pictures him in the light of the Jewish holidays and as a more modern version of both Esther and Judah Maccabee.

There is also the thorough-going Jewish content of, and materials in, the Gospels. They clearly show the rabbinic style of Yeshua's teachings, for example, his parables and midrashic homilies. In his discussions and interactions, Yeshua uses rabbinic forms of argumentation and utilizes rabbinic opinions. His teachings are structured in light of the Sabbath and holiday cycle of synagogue Scripture readings. All this provides very strong evidence for the Jewish authorship of each of the Gospels. It also presents insurmountable obstacles to the theory of later church creation and editing of the Yeshua story.

The material in the Gospels is very Jewish, so Jewish in fact, that the second-century Church would not have known much about it. Moreover, by the second century, the Church leaders had developed an anti-Jewish bias. The intense Jewishness of the Gospels lends credence to the fact that they were not written in the second century and provides further evidence for their authenticity, accuracy, and reliability.

However, given that the Gospels may have been written in the forties or fifties of the first century, that still leaves considerable time—perhaps even a few decades—between the events themselves and the records about them. That would seem to be enough time for inaccuracies to develop as the stories were told and retold. While it may be theoretically possible, the nature of education and oral transmission in Second Temple Judaism suggests otherwise.

Those in modern society often assume that the written transmission of materials is superior to their oral transmission. Written records would seem to prevent the kind of modification and distortion that often creeps into the retelling of stories and traditions. Therefore, it is often difficult to appreciate the reliability and precision that accompany oral transmission in societies accustomed to, and trained for, this form of communication and education. Before the advent of the printing press, written literature had to be hand copied to enable its wide circulation and distribution. When texts are hand copied, mistakes known as "copyist's errors" inevitably creep in. Given these circumstances, the accuracy of orally transmitted material clearly exceeded that of written material.

Although reading and writing were highly developed in Israel in the first century, written materials—especially religious literature—remained highly expensive. Trained scribes had to carefully copy these texts by hand, so the sacred scrolls were quite scarce. Consequently, learning required a significant amount of memorization. Of course, repetition was the key to this process, as the rabbis of the Talmud (a rabbinic compilation of principles, discussions, and decisions regarding behavior in keeping with the Torah) were quick to remind their students: "If one learns Torah and does not go over it again and again, he is like a man who sows without reaping" (Sanhedrin 99a). Through the use of memory aids and constant repetition, the people became quite good at memorizing extensive portions of material verbatim.

> The memorization of Written and Oral Law was such a large part of Jewish education that most contemporaries of Jesus had large portions of this material—at the least almost all of the Scriptures—firmly committed to memory. (Bivin 2)

The results and success of this orally-oriented education system laid the foundation for the accurate oral transmission of the religious traditions, both rabbinic and messianic.

Sociological and anthropological studies have been conducted of societies with an oral orientation. Such studies (for example, Ong's *Orality and Literacy*) have described and demonstrated how verbal accounts and historical events are orally transmitted over many generations with incredible precision and accuracy. Second Temple Israel was just such a society, as previously mentioned. Not only were the students of the first-century sages or rabbis instructed to engage in constant repetition to ensure the accurate memorization of their "lessons," they were warned to transmit them to others accurately. They were expressly prohibited from altering any of the words or teachings of their rabbis. They were told, in the words of the Talmud: "A person must always transmit a tradition in the same words in which he received it from his teacher" (*Eduyot* 1:3). This care and attentiveness, coupled with a sharply honed memory, produced the incredible preciseness of the Second Temple traditions and the gospel accounts.

The oral transmission of both narrative and didactic materials over many years can be completely trustworthy and historically accurate. And, this is particularly true when dealing with societies such as that of Second Temple Judaism—whose educational system is orally oriented. (Fischer, *Foundations* 80)

Therefore, the gospel accounts were not only written very early, but the events and conversations they record were orally passed on with great accuracy for the decade or so until they were committed to writing.

Are the Gospels Primary Historical Sources Containing Eyewitness Testimony?

The previous question dealt with the age and authenticity of the gospel records. This second question deals more specifically with their accuracy and veracity. When dealing with ancient literary sources, three standard tests are normally applied in order to determine the historical reliability of the documents under investigation. These tests are described in a number of sources (for example, Sanders, *Introduction to Research in English Literary History*, or Gottschalk, *Understanding History: A Primer of Historical Method*).

The Bibliographic Test

The first of these tests is often called the bibliographic test. It asks two questions: How many manuscript copies are there of the original document? How near are those manuscripts to the original itself?

In answering these questions about the Gospels of the Newer Testament, a series of comparisons may be helpful. The Newer Testament documents will be compared with two Greek historians (Herodotus and Thucydides) and two Roman historians (Livy and Tacitus). Herodotus (*History*) and Thucydides (*History*) both wrote about the time of Ezra the

Scribe (fifth century B.C.E.). Eight copies of each of those works exist today. The earliest copy in each case—with the exception of a few scraps—dates to approximately 900 C.E., a time span of over thirteen hundred years. Livy wrote *Roman History* about the time of Yeshua, while Tacitus wrote *Histories* at the end of the first century C.E. Twenty copies of Livy have been found, but only one copy of Tacitus has been discovered. The earliest copy of Livy—apart from a small fragment—comes from approximately 800 C.E., over eight hundred years after the original was written. The copy of Tacitus is dated between 900 and 1000 C.E., more than eight hundred years after Tacitus wrote. The works of Herodotus, Thucydides, Livy, and Tacitus are considered highly reliable.

In the case of the Gospels, the following holds true. Papyrus fragments of these texts date to the first century, perhaps as early as the mid to late sixties. (And, that doesn't include the numerous first-century quotations by Clement of Rome.) This leaves a span of some fifteen to fifty years between the original documents and the earliest copies. Over one hundred papyrus copies come from the beginning of the second century through the fourth, while the major complete manuscripts start appearing in the fourth and fifth centuries, a span of eighty to five hundred years after the originals. Another five thousand copies date from the fifth century on. In other words, both the number and the nearness of the manuscript copies far surpass what is available for the Greek and Roman historians. If those works are considered highly reliable, how much more so should the Gospels be regarded as trustworthy history?

The Internal Test

The second standard test for assessing historical reliability is the internal test. It asks three basic questions: Do the witnesses agree? Do they claim to be eyewitnesses? Do they qualify as eyewitnesses?

1. The first question raises the issue of potential contradiction or conflict among the different sources. It should be noted that the testimony of witnesses does not have to be uni-

form or identical. Often, identical testimony merely indicates collaboration among the witnesses rather than independent, first-hand testimony. Therefore, proper testimony centers on different areas from diverse perspectives, which converge and confirm one another. Details from numerous vantage points do not imply contradiction or conflict; they can be harmonized. In fact, a number of books have successfully harmonized the various gospel accounts. Cheney and Ellison have done this in *The Greatest Story.*

2. The second question relates to eyewitness claims made by the documents' authors. On numerous occasions, these authors claim to be eyewitnesses to the events they record.

> Concerning the matters that have taken place among us, many people have undertaken to draw up accounts based on what was handed down to us by those who from the start were eyewitnesses and proclaimers of the message. Therefore, Your Excellency, since I have carefully investigated these things from the beginning, it seemed good to me that I too should write you an accurate and ordered narrative. (Luke 1:1–3)

Luke asserts that both first-hand, eyewitness testimony and careful historical investigation underlie his account. Also, Yochanan (John) is quite adamant that his testimony is not just first-hand, but "up close and personal."

> We have heard him, we have seen him with our eyes, we have contemplated him, we have touched him with our hands! What we have seen and heard, we are proclaiming to you. (1 John 1:1, 3)

Others express this similarly.

> For when we made known to you the power and the coming of our Lord Yeshua the Messiah, we did not rely on cunningly contrived myths. On the contrary, we saw his majesty with our own eyes. For we were there. (1 Pet. 1:16–17)

Here, Shimon (Peter) reinforces Yochanan's claim that they were direct participants in the events they relate.

> For among the first things I passed on to you was what I also received, namely this: the Messiah died for our sins, in accordance with what the *Tanakh* says; and he was buried; and he was raised on the third day, in accordance with what the *Tanakh* says; and he was seen by Kefa, then by the Twelve; and afterwards, he was seen by more than five hundred brothers at one time, the majority of whom are still alive, though some have died. Later he was seen by Ya'akov [James], then by all the emissaries; and last of all he was seen by me. (1 Cor. 15:3–8)

Rav Shaul not only claims to be an eyewitness himself, but he also cites numerous others who were as well, including some 500+ people. Clearly, these authors not only claim to be eyewitnesses, but also first-hand participants in the events they report.

3. But, do they qualify as eyewitnesses? First, can the Gospels even be eyewitness accounts? Given the manuscript evidence already examined, they can. The early date of the manuscript copies, reinforced by the indications found within the texts themselves, all point to an early date of composition for the gospel accounts. In other words, the Gospels were written early enough to have been written by the actual eyewitnesses themselves. Second, what evidence do they give of being actual eyewitnesses? The evidence usually falls into three categories: incidental facts, textual objectivity, and cultural projection.

Incidental facts refer to the unimportant, or irrelevant details that are found in the texts which could be known only to eyewitnesses. These are included for no apparent purpose other than serving as part of the author's first-hand recollection of the events in which he participated. The Gospels give numerous examples of these.

Mark records the incident of the young man, who, at Yeshua's arrest, literally ran right out of his clothes and exited the scene naked (Mark 15:51–52). This detail could only have been known by an eyewitness. In fact, in those days, apart from the actual individual in question, no one else—out of consideration for the young man and his potential embarrassment—would have included it in the account.

Yochanan reports a very personal event. He tells of Yeshua handing over the responsibility for caring for his mother to Yochanan (John 19:26–27). This incident could only have been known to Yochanan and Miryam (Mary) herself.

Luke writes of the walk along the road to Emmaus (Luke 24:13–35). The precise details and exact conversation of that experience are communicated in a way that indicates that Luke himself participated in that exciting encounter.

Mattityahu (Matthew) describes Yeshua's invitation to be one of his students (Matt. 9:9–13). When the other Gospels record this incident, they name the tax collector, Levi, Mattityahu's less common Hebrew name, out of respect for his reputation. Tax collectors were despised by the people, so the other authors don't use the name by which he is more popularly known, Mattityahu. Only Mattityahu, himself, would retain the option of using his familiar name and "exposing" his shady past in this way, something only a personal participant in the events might choose to do.

The abundance of seemingly irrelevant, incidental details scattered throughout the gospel texts lends weight to the reliability of their accounts. These are just the kind of "picturesque" descriptions that normally characterize first person, eyewitness reports.

Textual objectivity refers to the portrayal of the protagonists and heroes by the texts themselves. How are the leading figures and respected leaders presented? Are they idealized and sanitized like the mythical heroes of ancient legends? Or, are they pictured as fallible humans plagued by shortcomings? As it turns out, the gospel records often give a rather negative view of those whom they hold in high esteem; embarrassing incidents are retained, as is, rather than cleaned up or whitewashed.

Shimon often comes across as quick to speak, but slow to understand. At a most crucial time, he denies his teacher repeatedly, and turns his back on him when confronted by a mere servant girl. Ya'akov, Yeshua's brother, not only refuses to follow Yeshua at the outset, he mocks and disdains him.

Yochanan's rage and temper prompt him to request instant fiery judgment on their opponents. He is certainly not a picture of compassion and consideration. Then there is Rav Shaul, Yeshua's foremost interpreter. He eagerly persecutes Yeshua's followers, and even requests the High Priest's permission to actively pursue them beyond the borders of Israel. He stands by callously while Stephen is stoned to death.

These are not the flattering portraits of heroes usually found in fables. Instead, they stand out as accurate descriptions of the flawed characters of history. These objective portrayals provide strong testimony to the trustworthiness of the texts. In addition, potentially conflicting minor details are not harmonized, nor are the difficult sayings or demanding standards of Yeshua glossed over or toned down for popular appeal. They are left as is. This further reinforces the integrity of the gospel accounts.

Cultural projection is a normal phenomenon that occurs when writers describe situations and circumstances from another place and time. Authors will often project their own values and viewpoints into the stories they record. This is not the case with the Gospels. They present a Yeshua who is completely at home within Judaism. He is firmly and comfortably rooted as a Jew, teaching the principles of Judaism, and commending its sages and teachers (cp. Matt. 5:18–21). The Gospels convey a high view of women. They are his full disciples and even function as leaders in his movement. The second-century non-Jewish world did not share these values and perspectives. In these circles, Judaism was demonized, and women were considered second class. The Gospels then do not exhibit the usual tendency found in authors writing long after the events. Their texts show no signs of the prevailing cultural viewpoints of the second century; they indicate the opposite—a first-century eyewitness report.

Before leaving this discussion of the internal test for a document's historical reliability, some reflection on the credibility of fishermen as eyewitnesses is worthwhile. Since their accounts form the core of the story about Yeshua, in some sense, part of the historical trustworthiness of the texts hinges on their credibility and character. So, what do we know about them? Were they ignorant working "stiffs" who couldn't be expected to remember exactly or report accurately, who couldn't help resorting to elaboration and invention? If this is the case, no confidence should be placed in their accounts.

In reality, at least in the first century, fishing was a very important, major industry in the Roman Empire (see Murphy-O'Connor, "Fishers of Men"). Fish was the major staple of the Near Eastern diet for both the rich and the poor. Far too frequently, the supply of fresh and smoked fish simply did not meet the demand. As a result, prices went up, and fishermen became quite wealthy. Fishing was "big business." Those who ran this business—if they were to succeed—had to be good businessmen. Bethsaida and Capernaum were just two of over a dozen significant seaports surrounding the Sea of Galilee, and Magdala may have been the central fish "factory," which processed the fish from these harbors.

The Gospels reveal that Shimon and Andrew, and Ya'akov and Yochanan, were owners of major fishing operations. They could come and go as they pleased; they controlled their own schedules and lives, indicating that they were men of wealth. This assessment is confirmed by the size and quality of Shimon's house in Capernaum; it is larger than most found in that city. In addition to their extensive education in the religious texts of Judaism, their business background and expertise ensured that they were practical and pragmatic, not gullible or ignorant. They had the training to report accurately, the intelligence to discern astutely. They were reliable, reputable, respected, and educated leaders in their community, and therefore qualified and credible eyewitnesses.

The External Test

The third test that is used to evaluate the historical trustworthiness of an ancient text is the external test. It, too, raises a few questions. Do other historical materials confirm the testimony of the document in question? What sources substantiate the text's authenticity and accuracy? Here there are three areas for investigation: the archaeological, the cultural, and the literary.

1. Albright summarized the situation for the Newer Testament quite well: "Discovery after discovery has established the accuracy of innumerable details" (*The Archaeology of Palestine* 127).

A couple of examples—out of numerous possibilities—should suffice. These are taken from Yochanan's gospel since it is often considered the latest and least historical of the four. John 19:13 mentions the "court" where Pilate tried Yeshua, and names it "Gabbatha," or Pavement. It was destroyed during the siege of Jerusalem in 70 C.E. and remained unknown and buried until the twentieth century. Critics faulted Yochanan for inventing the story. However, it has been excavated and identified—and can be viewed—as the court outside the Tower of Antonio. The healing story in John 5 describes that event as taking place at the Pool of Bethesda with its "five covered colonnades" (v. 2). It was another site with no other record of it, and so, it came under suspicion too. It was rediscovered, as described, just outside the Church of St. Anne in the Old City of Jerusalem. These archaeological discoveries substantiate the historical trustworthiness of the Newer Testament.

2. The cultural investigation of ancient texts tries to determine whether the documents describe the people and their society accurately. One of the most difficult tasks of the first-century authors was to identify the official titles of the rulers of the various kinds of Roman provinces correctly. Each province or colony had its own specific official designation. The ruler was given a different official title depending on the category of the colony he supervised. Since these colonies changed status quite frequently, keeping up with—as well as keeping track of—the changing titles of their rulers was a difficult task. Yet, Luke, who mentioned these officials repeatedly, never missed a beat. He got all the titles, provinces, and people right each time. This was such a daunting task that the renowned archaeologist Sir William Ramsay—originally, a confirmed skeptic and critic himself—remarked: "Luke is a historian of the first rank . . . this author should be placed with the very greatest of historians" (222).

Other recent discoveries have helped further the cultural examination of the Gospels, specifically with regard to their portrayal of the religious practices and climate of the times they describe. In the late 1940s two important ancient libraries were discovered: the "cave library" of the Qumran community, also known as the Dead Sea Scrolls, and the Gnostic library of Nag Hammadi in Egypt. While the former is far better known, the latter is equally significant. The Scrolls describe an important part of Judaism that spans the time from the Maccabees to the destruction of the Second Temple (c.150 B.C.E. to 70 C.E.). The Gnostic library illumines an important Judeo-Christian stream of religious thought that emerges in the late first and early second centuries C.E. One frequent critique of the Gospels, especially Yochanan, was that it derived from the Gnostic and Hellenistic world of the second century.

With the discoveries of these two libraries, much more is known of both the Jewish world prior to the destruction of the Temple and of the Gnostic world at the turn of the first century—and they are two quite distinct outlooks. A comparison of the two libraries with the Gospels shows that the Gospels breathe the air of the pre-destruction world of Judaism, not that of the second-century world of Gnosticism. In other words, what they actually describe is, in fact, what they claim to describe, the early first-century Jewish world of Yeshua, and they do so with minute precision and accuracy. As Kistemacher points out in his summary of this discussion, the comparison of the Gospels with the Qumran and Nag Hammadi libraries clearly places the Gospels squarely "in the context of Palestinian Judaism, not in first-century Hellenism or second-century Gnosticism" (Kistemacher 129).

A comparison of the Gospels with the rabbinic materials and with the apocryphal literature arising from the time between the Testaments yields similar results. The Gospels reflect an outlook and culture that is shaped by the same theological developments and religious thought that produced the Apocrypha. (See, for example, Fujita, *A Crack in the Jar.*) And, they are also stamped by the ongoing rabbinic traditions and discussions from the time of Ezra to the Talmud. (See, for example, Lachs, *A Rabbinic Commentary on the New Testament.*) Therefore, it is not surprising to find that, throughout his teaching, Yeshua continually uses rabbinic argumentation and alludes to established rabbinic opinions. The cultural test confirms the reliability of the gospel documents.

3. The last external test for determining the historic trust-worthiness of the materials is the literary. This examines whether references in other literature align with the texts in question when they describe similar events. F. F. Bruce deals with these in detail in *Jesus and Christian Origins Outside the New Testament*. A few citations should be sufficient at this point.

The Roman author Thallus, writing about 52 C.E., mentions the same situation described by the Gospels: "On the whole world there pressed a fearful darkness; and the rocks were rent by an earthquake, and many places in Judea and other districts were thrown down" (Julius Africanus, *Chronologies*, qtd. in Bruce, *Documents*, 113). Josephus was a Jewish historian who served as a general in the first revolt against Rome (66–70 C.E.). He wrote:

> Now there was about this time a very wise man . . . a doer of many marvelous works, a teacher of such men who receive the truth with pleasure. He won over to him both many of the Jews and many of the Gentiles. . . . And when Pilate, at the suggestion of the principal men among us, had condemned him to the cross, those that loved him at the first did not forsake him. For he appeared to them alive again the third day. (*Antiquities* 18.3.3)

Hence, other literature of the day confirmed the material in the Newer Testament. In fact, all three lines of examination that serve as part of the external test converge to show that the Gospels are clearly corroborated by outside archaeological, cultural and literary sources. They are trustworthy historical documents.

This chapter's second question raised and examined the issue of whether the Gospels are primary historical sources, containing first-hand eyewitness testimony. The three standard tests for assessing the historical reliability of ancient tests, when applied to the Gospels, certainly indicate the Gospels are historically trustworthy accounts. It should be clear, then, that the Gospels are, in fact, reliable. They were written not long after the events they describe. Moreover, the accuracy of oral transmission during this time further guarantees that the communication of information was entirely reliable and historically trustworthy. Applying the research methods for testing the authenticity of ancient documents adds to the reliability of the Newer Testament documents, particularly the Gospels. This is important since what the Gospels really say about the relationship between Yeshua and the Jewish people has been distorted for 2000 years. This leads to the next issue, the distortion that the Gospels are anti-Semitic.

✡　✡　✡

For Further Reading

Barnett, Paul. *Is the New Testament Reliable?* InterVarsity Press.

Blomberg, Craig. *The Historical Reliability of the Gospels.* InterVarsity Press.

Bruce, F.F. *The New Testament Documents: Are they Reliable?* InterVarsity Press.

Ewen, P.B. *Faith on Trial.* Broadman and Holman.

Greenleaf, Simon. *The Testimony of the Evangelists as Examined by the Laws of Evidence Administered in Courts of Justice.* Baker Books.

Ramsay, Sir W.M. *The Bearing of Recent Discovery on the Trustworthiness of the New Testament.* Hodder and Stoughton.

Robinson, J.A.T. *The Priority of John.* Westminster Press.

Robinson, J.A.T. *Redating the New Testament.* Westminster Press.

Wenham, John. *Redating Matthew, Mark and Luke.* InterVarsity Press.

Chapter 2

Are the Gospels Anti-Semitic?

Once again, Mel Gibson's film, *The Passion of the Christ*, raises a question about the Gospels: "Are the Gospels Anti-Semitic?" After all, isn't their treatment of Jews blatantly negative and intentionally hostile? Aren't the Jews held personally responsible for the death of Yeshua and portrayed as the enemies of God?" The answer has profound ramifications, not only for the ethical integrity of the gospel message, but also for the appropriate response to religious anti-Semitism. Further, if the Gospels themselves are anti-Semitic, and Gibson's intent was to present an unadulterated version of the Gospels, any anti-Semitism that might be reflected in the movie is not ultimately Mel Gibson's fault, but rather the gospel authors'.

History has sufficiently demonstrated that the Newer Testament has, in fact, been repeatedly quoted by anti-Semites and employed for anti-Semitic purposes. From the second-century Marcionites—who considered the Jews, their Scriptures, and their God as evil—to early church leaders—who urged the hatred of Jews—to the Czarists and Nazis—who provided religious reasons for persecuting and exterminating Jews—anti-Semites have manipulated the Gospels for their own purposes. From the Middle Ages to the Modern Age, Passion Plays have been at the forefront of this problem. Even Hitler was quoted as saying, after leaving a Passion Play in 1934: "The whole world over should see this Passion Play; then they will understand why I despise the Jews and why they deserve to die" (Mork 157). But are the Gospels at the root of the problem?

On closer examination, the core issue is really whether the Gospels are, in fact, anti-Semitic; or, is it just that they have been interpreted anti-Semitically? The reasonable and informed reader would certainly not expect Jews to be anti-Semitic. After all, the Gospels were written by Jews! As was noted earlier, "Every book of the New Testament was written by a baptized Jew" (Albright, *Christianity Today* 18). Therefore, it would be natural to assume that the problem is indeed one of interpretation. As the Catholic scholar Gregory Baum emphatically pointed out:

> There is no foundation for the accusation that a seed of contempt and hatred for the Jews can be found in the New Testament . . . no degradation of the Jewish people, no unjust accusation, no malevolent prophecy is ever suggested or implied. (qtd. in Flannery 30–31)

The highly regarded Jewish scholar, Louis Feldman, concurs: "My own examination of the New Testament has led me to the conclusion that, taken as a whole, it is not antisemitic" (Feldman 32). Hence, when read contextually and culturally, the Gospels are not anti-Semitic. They do not describe Jews as a group, or Jews as a people to be evil or inferior. Therefore, a number of important passages need to be re-examined in light of this assessment.

Tough-Sounding Texts

At the outset, it should be recognized that there are numerous occasions where Yeshua, and later Rav Shaul and the other apostles, find themselves in situations of conflict with some of the religious leadership. For example, in Thessalonica (Acts 17:5–9) and Achaia (Acts 18:12–17) the religious leadership attacks Jews who responded positively to Shaul's message. The accounts recording these incidents cannot be considered anti-Semitic. They merely reported the actions of certain Jews in leadership; they did not speak of all Jews or Jews as a group.

The gospel records are similar. They describe Yeshua as in conflict with some of the official leaders from Jerusalem and the Sanhedrin (for example, Matt. 15:1–10; 16:1–4); they do not portray him as opposed to the Jewish people, in general.

In point of fact, Jews are consistently presented in a positive light. Therefore, Shaul emphatically declares:

> God has by no means rejected his people (Rom. 11:1–2). They are dearly loved for the sake of their ancestors, and the call of God on them is irrevocable (Rom. 11:28–29). The advantage of the Jew is much in every way (Rom. 3:1–2).

Further, the Gospels indicate that Torah teachers followed Yeshua (for example, Matt. 8:19), and synagogue leaders trusted him (Matt. 9:18). Pharisees tried to protect him from Herod (Luke 13:31), and Scribes are mentioned as examples to follow (Matt. 13:52). Yeshua even used the Pharisees as standards of piety (Matt. 5:20), and he instructed his disciples to follow their teachings (Matt. 23:2–3). As for the Jewish crowds, the Gospels regularly point out their avid and enthusiastic interest in Yeshua and his teachings (Mark 12:37). In fact, it is Yeshua's popularity with these Jewish masses that hinders the Sanhedrin in its attempt to do away with him (Matt. 26:3–4). For the gospel writers, Jews are not enemies; they are friends.

One of the "suspect" descriptions (of anti-Semitism) is that of the Jews as "killers of the prophets" (for example, Matt. 23:37). Yet, this phrase seems quite common in the Jewish literature of the day in describing rebellious leaders, and is frequent in the rabbinic materials as well (for example, *Exodus Rabba* 48.3; *Yevamot* 49b; *Gittin* 57b). It denounces those specific people (usually leaders) who oppose God, and is not aimed at the larger group. The Gospels follow this same pattern, focusing their critique on opposition within the religious hierarchy, not on the Jewish people, as a whole.

Matthew 23, with its stinging denunciation of the Pharisees, probably stands out as the most problematic of the troublesome texts. Yeshua describes them as "hypocrites" and a "brood of vipers," among other things. Yet, contemporary treatments of the Pharisees, written by Pharisees themselves, also speak of hypocrites in similarly harsh tones. They write: "Let ravens peck out the eyes of the hypocrites" (Psalms of Solomon 4:22; cp. *Yevamot* 63b). Another tractate of the Talmud (*Sotah* 20a–22b) reads: "The plague of the Pharisees brings destruction on the world." That plague is defined as hypocrisy, and described behavior similar to that which Yeshua denounces. The "shoulder" Pharisee, for example, wears his piety on his shoulders for all to see (cp. Matt. 23:3–4). In fact, of the seven types of Pharisees found in the Talmudic text, only two are considered good. The ongoing complaint in the text is over ostentatious piety and insincere motivation. An ancient rabbinic commentary on the biblical texts, the *Midrash Rabba* elaborates on the same problem.

> Everyone thinks he is a scholar of Torah but he is not. He wraps himself in his tallit [prayer shawl] and puts the tefillin [phylacteries] on his head, and yet he oppresses the poor. . . . The Holy One, blessed be He, says, "I will punish him," as it is said, "Cursed is he that does the work of the Lord deceitfully." [Jer. 48:10] (*Kohelet Rabba* 4:1)

Yeshua's condemnation of the hypocrites among the Pharisees parallels that of some of the writing of the Pharisees themselves. The tone of the rabbinic writings is no less harsh than that of the Gospels. The Talmud and the Midrash (a collection of rabbinic homilies, on and elaboration of, the Scriptures) are both ultimately the products of the Pharisees. So, rabbinic/Pharisaic literature employs the same imagery and harsh criticism as the Gospels in condemning the same problems. In words almost identical to Yeshua's (Luke 12:1–2), the Talmud states: "What is hidden is hidden, and what is revealed is revealed; the Great Judgment will exact punishment on those who behave hypocritically" (*Sotah* 22b).

Even Yeshua's exceptionally harsh description of the leaders as "sons of the devil" (John 8:44) turns out to be rather unexceptional. The first-century sage, Rabbi Dosa ben Harkinas, criticized his brother Jonathan for a ruling that was in line with the teachings of Beth Shammai, one of the major rabbinic schools of thought in the late Second Temple period. As part of his scathing criticism of his brother's decision, the rabbi calls him "the firstborn of Satan" (*Yevamot* 16a). Phrases such as serpents, brood of vipers, sons of the devil, and firstborn of Satan were part of the vocabulary of the sometimes heated discussions over matters of appropriate religious practice. Yeshua's critique, and the Gospels' descriptions, form a part of the same internal discourse; they share the same passion of the ongoing family debates.

A Mis-Applied Text

Another very troubling passage is Matthew 27:25, "His blood be on us and on our children." Perhaps, no passage has been used more frequently to justify social or theological anti-Semitism than this text. It has been used to prove that the Jews took on themselves the guilt of killing Yeshua, and so stand eternally liable for divine judgment. Yet, it is highly instructive that even those early church leaders who were vehemently anti-Jewish did *not* cite this passage in their writings. They apparently did not view this text as a general indictment of the Jews, as did later generations of anti-Semites. That indicates that there is a significant issue here about the proper interpretation of this incident.

The first thing that should be noted at this point is the location of this encounter. Yochanan calls it *Gabbatha* (John 19:13), the stone pavement or court in front of Pilate's official residence, the Tower of Antonio. This area has been excavated, as noted earlier. It would have accommodated a little over one hundred people. During holiday times, such as Passover when this was said, Jerusalem usually contained about a quarter of a million Jews. Hence, only one hundred people out of a quarter million in the city made this inflammatory statement.

They certainly did not, and could not, speak for the large crowds elsewhere in the city. They by no means spoke for the large numbers of Jews throughout Israel, who were not in Jerusalem at that time (perhaps a million people). And, that doesn't include the large majority (well over three-quarters) of Jews who were living outside the land of Israel at the end of the first century. Obviously, and logically, then, it seems rather absurd to apply this statement—made by only one hundred people—to the Jewish people as a whole. The Gospels certainly don't intend it that way, even if the few Jews in the court actually did say those words.

The meaning and implications of this statement also bear further examination. There is a similar text in Acts 18:6, where Rav Shaul exclaims, in exasperation, "Your blood be on your own heads!" Was his statement intended to call a blood curse down upon the Jews? Not at all! The statement merely indicates, though stated quite descriptively, that the Jewish leaders of Corinth were responsible for their actions. The phrase functions similarly in Matthew 27. Pilate, taunting the Sanhedrin, pretends to absolve himself from the responsibility of ordering Yeshua's execution. (Incidentally, no Roman governor could legally or practically absolve himself in this fashion, and then let others carry out an execution, without violating Roman law.) The priests refuse to take the bait and lead the response, "So, we'll be responsible then." Both they and Pilate knew that was impossible by Roman law. Then, Pilate orders the execution.

Theologically, there is more here, as well. At his final Passover seder, Yeshua connected his "blood" with the ratification of the new covenant, the Covenant of Renewal (Matt. 26:28). (For a development of the renewal emphasis of this covenant, see Fischer, "Covenant, Fulfillment, and Judaism in Hebrews" in *The Enduring Paradox*.) The blood associated with any ancient Near Eastern covenant—as also the blood associated with the Temple sacrifices, including the Passover sacrifice—had to be "innocent blood." Only "innocent blood" makes restoration to God possible. Without it, there can be no real forgiveness theologically, and no intimate relationship personally. The gospel writers make the definite point, especially through Pilate's "role-playing" about Yeshua's innocence, that this was "innocent blood" indeed, and therefore, was properly qualified to be an effective sacrifice. In other words, Yeshua's blood was to be shed for a special purpose—a renewal of the covenant.

Another aspect of this sacrificial imagery is reflected in the grammatical construction of the statement, "His blood be on us." The Greek word for "on," *epi*, as also the Hebrew behind it, *al*, can mean "over us," as with a covering. In this case, the gospel writer structures the leaders' response to Pilate, so as to make an important theological statement: Yeshua's "innocent blood" would provide atonement; it would cover sin. And that, of course, is exactly what Yeshua meant, and Matthew underscores, in Matthew 26:28: "My blood will be poured out for many for the forgiveness of sin." Far from being understood as a curse, this passage should be culturally and contextually understood as a powerful image of the perfect sacrifice.

Here, the literary imagery is a reminder of the story of Rebekah and Jacob. Rebekah volunteers to take responsibility for Jacob's actions (Gen. 27:13). An informed reader, knowledgeable in the Scriptures, would have made the connection to Rebekah's statement, assuming responsibility. It is vitally important to note, neither Rebekah nor Jacob was ever "cursed" by either Isaac or God. In this case, then, Matthew would have his readers realize that those making the statement about Yeshua's blood were not cursed by God either, because Yeshua bore the curse. This is precisely the point made later by Rav Shaul. He states, citing Deuteronomy 21:23, that "anyone hung on a tree is under God's curse." He then adds that Yeshua "rescued us from this curse, by taking this curse on himself" (Gal. 3:13). That is Matthew's point here as well, though conveyed through literary imagery. There is no curse on Jews to be found in Matthew 27:25.

Do the Gospels Really Say That the Jews Killed Yeshua?

This discussion raises the issue of who bears responsibility for the death of Yeshua, an important point in view of the recurring accusation that "the Jews killed Christ." Its ramifications are reinforced by what one Holocaust survivor related that she saw as she entered one of the notorious death camps. She encountered a sign which read, "You are here because you killed our God." The biblical perspective is highly instructive.

Acts 4:27 reads: "In this city, Herod and Pontius Pilate, with the Goyim [Gentiles] and the people of Israel, assembled against your holy servant Yeshua, whom you made Messiah." Scripture clearly indicts the leaders—interestingly, both appointed by Rome—and then the Gentiles, and then the people of Israel, and in that order. Yeshua himself said his execution would take place in the following way: "The Son of Man will be betrayed to the chief priests and the teachers of the law. They will condemn him to death and will turn him over to the Gentiles to be mocked and flogged and crucified" (Matt. 20:18–19). In other words, Judas would betray him to the Jewish leaders comprising the Sanhedrin, who would sentence him to death and turn him over to the Roman authorities. These Gentiles would taunt, flog, and execute him. By the way, in Acts 3:17, Shimon points out that the Jewish leaders, and the Jews involved, acted out of ignorance.

It should also be noted that pious Pharisees in leadership would have only two choices concerning Yeshua, given his claims to deity. They could accept him as the supernatural Messiah, or they could condemn him for blasphemy; Yeshua left them no other choice. Nicodemus and Joseph and numerous others were among those who acknowledged him, but there were those who felt they had to oppose him because of his claims.

On the other hand, the Sadducees had a different agenda, as indicated by John 11:49–50; 18:13–14. Caiaphas and the other chief priests served at the will and whim of Rome. If there was any political turmoil among the Jews, as leaders, they would be held responsible. It would be to their benefit, then, as Caiaphas pointed out, that "one man die for the nation, rather than the whole nation [read: "their leadership"] perish." Yeshua was a threat—due to his immense popularity among the people (Matt. 26:3–4)—to their political power.

Interestingly, Luke 18:31–33 omits the Sanhedrin's part entirely and mentions only the Gentiles, perhaps to emphasize the primary role and responsibility of the Gentiles/

Romans for the death of Yeshua. Rav Shaul also emphasizes the role of the Gentiles when he says: "Not one of this world's leaders understood it; because if they had, they would not have executed the Lord" (1 Cor. 2:8). Here, Gentile leaders are held accountable for Yeshua's death, although they, too, acted out of ignorance.

So, the Newer Testament clearly does not "pick on" the Jews as primarily responsible for Yeshua's death. In fact, it gives equal or greater prominence to the Gentiles' role in his execution. Even when it discusses the Jewish role in the process, it focuses attention on the official religious hierarchy centered in Jerusalem. Furthermore, concerning those who were involved, Yeshua's request should be clearly noted: "Father, forgive them, for they do not know what they are doing" (Luke 23:34). This request was most certainly granted! According to the Gospels, then, "the Jews did *not* kill Christ!"

Pilate's Role in Yeshua's Death

Pilate's role in Yeshua's death has been presented in different ways. Quite frequently, he is seen as a beleaguered Roman official, wanting to follow his wife's warnings about Yeshua's innocence, but forced by the Jewish leaders to have him executed. He sincerely wants the truth about Yeshua, but the cries of the crowd force his hand. This is a very sympathetic and flattering portrait of this important figure. Unfortunately, this is not the Pilate of history, and more to the point, it is not the Pilate of the Gospels.

Among the seven prefects who held office as governors of Judea, Pilate is the one discussed in most detail in historical writings. Philo and Josephus are among those who describe his term of office. The Pilate known to historians is unbending, harsh, and stubborn; his actions are cruel, vindictive, and greedy. They tell us he is famous for such things as corruption, violence, repeated executions without trial, and "endless and intolerable cruelties." He treats Jews and Jewish customs with the utmost contempt. Just to spite their religious sensibilities, he audaciously parades the Roman garrisons through Jerusalem, flaunting their banners bearing idolatrous images. In various protests, Jews were killed, and hatred against Pilate grew. Finally, his vindictiveness and recklessness caused his downfall. He ordered a vicious attack on a Samaritan village, resulting in the lodging of a formal complaint before Vitellius, the Syrian legate. Vitellius ordered him to Rome, where he was promptly removed from his position of authority. According to history, Pilate did not leave behind a positive legacy or an endearing portrait.

The Pilate pictured in the Gospels is no different. Here, too, he is seen as vicious and cruel. Using rather graphic imagery, Luke presents the Pilate "who mixed the blood of the Galileans with their sacrifices" (Luke 13:1). This is the historical Pilate, the Pilate of the Gospels, who occupies center stage as judge and executioner at Yeshua's trial. So, the reading and interpretation of his statements and actions at that encounter must be consistent with this accurate portrait, and not with a distortion.

When understood against this historical background, the Pilate who appears in the closing scenes of the Gospels can clearly be seen as mean-spirited, malicious, and manipulative. [The following discussion is based on a compilation and summary of all four gospel accounts.] When Yeshua is brought before him, he insultingly inquires as to the charges against him. Having no real love for Pilate, the priests give their sarcastic response: "If he weren't a criminal, he wouldn't be here!" Not to be outdone, Pilate cynically answers: "Then take him and judge him yourselves" (John 18:30, 31), knowing full well that they have no power to do that. Only Pilate has the authority to condemn and execute a person, and he provocatively reminds them of this. When he interrogates Yeshua, his responses are equally disdainful, contemptuous, and insincere. "Am I a Jew?" (John 18:35) would only be uttered with contempt by this arrogant Roman official. For this man, for whom truth and justice meant little when compared with force and the brutal display of power, "What is truth?" did not reflect a sincere philosophical quest. It communicated his disdain for that entire endeavor; why waste time on some stupid pursuit of truth? And, he personally doesn't!

To further provoke and enrage the priests, he announces his "verdict": "This man is not guilty." When they howl in protest, much to his delight, he continues to insult them publicly, offering them a choice between Yeshua and Barabbas. He knew of their feelings about Yeshua, but Barabbas was a convicted insurrectionist and murderer. He had tried to incite the city against its leaders (the priests of the Sanhedrin) and had killed those who supported their leadership. Pilate would never have knowingly released someone who would have been a danger to Rome. If he had, he would have placed himself in danger of Caesar's retaliation. Barabbas was particularly distasteful to the priests because of his actions against them. So Pilate cunningly and cruelly offers them a humiliating choice, Yeshua or Barabbas. They had invested a lot of their public "capital" and prestige in bringing each of these threats to trial; now Pilate maliciously forces the priests to "request" that one of these "public enemies" go free. When they make their humiliating request for Barabbas, he taunts them further by repeating their painful choice: "So, again, which of the two do you want me to release?" He is forcing them to repeat their request, this time even louder, as it were. Enjoying this game thoroughly, Pilate mockingly says: "But why? What has he done? I'll just punish him and release him!" Incidentally, if Pilate was really interested in truth and justice, and genuinely considered Yeshua innocent, he would not—in good conscience—have ordered him flogged and scourged, which he then commanded.

However, Pilate is not yet done with the priests. To infuriate them further, he mockingly presents them with their beaten and bloodied "king." This insult operates on two levels. First, he knows they do not recognize him as their king, so he taunts them by saying that he is their king. Second, by presenting Yeshua in a mock purple robe and a crown made of thorns, he disparagingly shows them what he thinks of Jewish kings in general.

Relishing his advantage, Pilate continues his charade. He sits Yeshua down on the judge's seat and says, "Here's your king!" (John 19:13–14). He has now publicly and tauntingly "enthroned" Yeshua before their eyes. And then he jeeringly asks again: "You want me to execute your king on a stake?" Their reply is exactly what Pilate wants to hear from them: "We have no king but the Emperor" (John 19:15).

Two things need to be said about this reply. First, being the priests of the Sanhedrin, they had long before, willingly and wholeheartedly acknowledged this fact. As Sadducees, they were philosophically and pragmatically committed to Roman rule. Second, by manipulating them to repeat this in public, Pilate was forcing them to acknowledge, in a humiliating fashion, that he was the one in charge.

Having accomplished his purpose, Pilate diabolically continues his public ridicule and humiliation of the priests. He washes his hands. The priests had to wash their hands at the laver (basin) in the Temple courtyard before they could offer the sacrifices. Mocking their revered practices, Pilate flauntingly washes his hands, indicating that he is about to preside at a sacrifice. This ridicule is enhanced because he knew Jews were revolted by human sacrifice, which is exactly what he was about to mockingly perform. However, Mattityahu clearly intends his readers to see that, despite Pilate's ridicule, Yeshua *is* dying as a sacrifice of atonement in keeping with passages such as Isaiah 53. Then, after releasing Barabbas to further incite the priests, and showing absolutely no remorse over or concern for Yeshua, Pilate again hands Yeshua over to his soldiers for further beating and mocking. Pilate puts the finishing touches on his vicious and malicious "show" by placing the sign over Yeshua's cross. The sign effectively says: "This is what Rome does to Jewish kings!"

It is clear that a vicious, cruel Pilate, fulfilling his general hostility toward Jews and Yeshua, was responsible for his death, *not* the Jewish people.

Did Yeshua Get a Fair Trial From the Sanhedrin?

Before concluding this section, Yeshua's "trial" before the Sanhedrin warrants some attention. The leaders of the Sanhedrin are frequently accused of operating illegally, according to their own rules, when they examine Yeshua. In other words, Yeshua did not receive a "fair trial" from the Jews.

As indicated by the politically-charged statements of the High Priest (John 11:49–50), the leadership viewed Yeshua as a potentially-destructive (at least to their own status) political subversive. They needed to determine if he could be viewed as a sufficient public threat to formally charge him before Pilate. Since they did not have the authority to crucify him (John 18:31), the rules regarding capital crimes cases did not apply. Instead, the Sanhedrin was functioning more like a grand jury inquiry, investigating whether there was ample evidence to charge Yeshua. Acting as a grand jury, rather than a formal legal court, the Sanhedrin broke no rules.

Because there had been numerous political disturbances associated with the Temple throughout Jewish history, Yeshua's statements about "destroying this Temple" alarmed the Sanhedrin. This marked him as a clear threat to public order, especially in the politically-charged atmosphere of the Passover holiday. Another Temple riot would result in Roman military reprisals and the end of the current High Priest's power. So Caiaphas asked Yeshua the "political" question: "Are you the Messiah?" The Messiah anticipated by Judaism would rule as king over Israel; he would be a political leader. Caiaphas reinforces the political nature of his question by adding the phrase "Son of the Blessed One" to his question. According to Psalm 2, and because of God's promises to David in 2 Samuel 7 and Psalm 89, "Son of God" became a title that referred to Israel's designated royal heir, a clearly political office. Yeshua's response provided the ammunition Caiaphas needed. He not only responded by saying "I am," he added "You will see the Son of Man seated at the right hand of the Mighty One, riding the clouds of heaven." In saying this, Yeshua combined Daniel 7:13–14 with Psalm 110:1 to claim supreme sovereignty. He not only claimed royalty, he claimed deity. And so, the High Priest responded: "We have no need of further witnesses; we have heard blasphemy!" The decision was now easy. There was ample evidence to charge Yeshua publicly and politically; he deserved death. Therefore, they brought him to trial before Pilate.

In the first-century Roman world, crucifixion was the mode of capital punishment reserved for political insurgents who threatened imperial rule. This is the unjust death sentence Pilate deliberately chose to impose on Yeshua.

The Derogatory Use of the Phrase, "The Jews"

The Newer Testament, and particularly the Gospels, is frequently cited for the derogatory treatment of Jews in its pages. Frequently, this is presented as evidence of its anti-Semitic bias. Yet, the prophets of Israel often forcefully critiqued the Jewish people of their own time when they turned away from God and the Torah, and did so in very strong terms. They are not considered anti-Semitic.

Jeremiah 23:9–15 is one such example. Verse 10 calls the people of the Land "adulterers." Their prophets and priests are described as "profane" (v. 11). Jeremiah then accuses their "prophets" of numerous crimes (v. 14). They commit adultery; they walk in lies; they strengthen evil people. Then, he compares them to the infamous evil cities Sodom and Gomorrah. Other prophets, like Isaiah, and especially Amos, issued similar charges. What occurred was one Jew—a prophet—critiquing other Jews —the Nation. This can hardly be called anti-Semitism.

This prophetic model often underlies the derogatory use of the phrase "the Jews" in the Gospels. Yochanan seems quite prone to this. However, on closer examination he uses the phrase in a number of ways and with a variety of meanings. He employs it to describe Yeshua's audience, who is friendly and receptive (John 8:31; 11:45; 12:11), or of the religious authorities who are neutral and inquisitive (John 1:19; 6:52).

In the passages describing the controversy between Yeshua and the religious hierarchy, the term usually refers to antagonistic Pharisees (John 5:16), or to the priestly establishment or Sanhedrin (John 18:12; 19:12–15). Since these specific individuals are viewed as in opposition to God and his Messiah, they are naturally and contextually cast in an unfavorable light. This is no more anti-Semitic than the prophets' statements.

The historical and cultural background of this gospel provides further insight into its usage of the phrase "the Jews." Yochanan, and many of Yeshua's other disciples, came from the Galilee. The inhabitants of Jerusalem and Judea, and especially the religious hierarchy, often ridiculed the Galileans for their perceived religious and social crudeness. So, for the Galileans, applying the term "the Jews" in a somewhat ironic and sarcastic way to their more self-assured and smugly religious "Judean" counterparts would be customary. In fact, *ioudaioi,* the Greek term used in these cases, literally means "Judeans." Hence, its use by Yochanan may be intentionally specific and technically precise. This term has been incorrectly translated as "Jews" in all versions of the Bible (except for the *Complete Jewish Bible*), contributing to the distortion.

Furthermore, this gospel is similar in language and thought to the writings of the Dead Sea Scroll community of Qumran. Many of their scrolls include vigorous protests against the Temple priesthood and the religious establishment, who are viewed as quite corrupt and in rebellion against God. Drawn from a similar background and perspective (see Morris, *Studies in the Fourth Gospel*). John's gospel shares a common criticism of the religious leadership and its shortcomings.

Several passages shed light on John's use of the phrase, "the Jews." John 7:10–13 describes Yeshua's appearance in Jerusalem at the holiday of Sukkot (Festival of Tabernacles or Booths). Verse 11 mentions "the Jews" while verse 12 describes the crowds. Here, the text views the crowds as distinct from "the Jews." Yet, most certainly, at this Jewish festival in Jerusalem, the crowds are as Jewish as "the Jews." Hence, "the Jews" refers to the Judean religious hierarchy in Jerusalem (v. 13).

John 9:13–22 describes the aftermath of Yeshua's healing of the blind man at this holiday in Jerusalem. Verses 16–18 mention "some Pharisees" as part of "the Jews." Verse 22 indicates that the blind man's parents are afraid of "the Jews." However, the parents were Jewish themselves! Why would they be afraid? Because "the Jews" might throw them out of the synagogue. Only the official religious leadership had this power. This indicates that the phrase "the Jews" refers to the religious hierarchy or official leadership, not to the Jewish people in general.

At this point, it should be noted that Rav Shaul's usage of the term "the Jews" in Acts 28:17–20, parallels John's usage. He uses the phrase to refer to the religious establishment, especially centered in Jerusalem. It refers to the Sanhedrin and its religious hierarchy, particularly its Sadducean leadership.

Clearly, the gospel accounts are not anti-Semitic. They stand firmly within the Jewish prophetic and rabbinic traditions. In fact, if anything, the Newer Testament—properly understood and interpreted—elevates and honors the Jewish people and their place in the program of God. Unfortunately, many readers of the Gospels—Jews and Christians—failed to grasp the positive relationship between Yeshua and the Jewish people. This misunderstanding quickly found its way into the history of the early church.

✿　✿　✿

For Further Reading

Baum, Gregory. *Is the New Testament Anti-Semitic?* Paulist Press.

Bock, Darrell. *Jesus According to Scripture.* Baker Books.

Bock, Darrell. "Jesus Versus the Sanhedrin." *Christianity Today.* (April 6, 1998): 47–50.

Bruce, F.F. "Are the Gospels Anti-Semitic?" *Eternity* (1973).

Cargal, Timothy. "'His Blood Be upon Us and upon Our Children': A Matthean Double Entendre?" *New Testament Studies* 37 (1991): 101–12.

Carroll, John, and Green, Joel. *The Death of Jesus in Early Christianity.* Hendrickson Publishers.

Feldman, Louis. "Is the New Testament Antisemitic?" *Moment* (December 1990): 32–35, 50–52.

LaSor, William. "'The Jews' in the Fourth Gospel," *Yavo Digest* 3 (no. 4, 1989).

Lee, Bernard. *The Galilean Jewishness of Jesus.* Paulist Press.

Lowe, Malcom. "Who Are the *Ioudaioi?*" *Novum Testamentum* XVIII (April 1976).

Vermes, Geza. *Jesus the Jew.* Collins.

Chapter 3

Has the Church Been Anti-Semitic?

There is an old Hasidic story about a student who goes to his rabbi and enthusiastically says, "Master, I love you!"

The rabbi responds with a perceptive question, "Tell me, do you know what hurts me?"

The bewildered young man is completely shaken. "Why do you ask me such a confusing question when I have just told you I love you?"

The old rabbi slowly shakes his head. "Because, my friend, if you do not know what really *hurts* me, how can you truly love me?"

The rabbi's wise question pertains to the question at hand. Who would think that people who follow the Messiah of Israel and the God of the Jewish Scriptures could hate Jews? Yet, some events of history have been hurtful.

A Brief History Christian Anti-Semitism

A genuine understanding of Jewish people—especially their re-action to things "Christian"—and a sincere and open relation-ship with them, requires at least a summary knowledge of the history of contact between the Church and the Jews.

In the Roman Empire, Moses was considered a seducer and a wizard, and the Torah was described as evil and dangerous. Since they did not worship any "visible" gods (idols and stat-ues), Jews were considered atheists who despised the gods and rejected religion. They were accused of being descended from lepers and of worshiping the head of a jackass. One of Nero's tutors even taught that Jews used human blood as part of their sacrificial rites.

Tertullian, the late second- and early third-century church leader vehemently attacked Jewish practices such as circumcision and Sabbath observance. Another second-century leader, Justin Martyr, used his book, *Dialogue with Trypho*, to undermine the legitimacy of Judaism's beliefs. In his writings, Origen also expressed hostility towards Jews and Judaism (Flannery 40–41).

Constantine built on these religious foundations and began enacting restrictions against the Jewish people, even making Christianity the Roman Empire's official religion. The attacks by Tertullian laid the foundation for the prohibitions enacted by Constantine (Parkes 11). These laws soon became increasingly oppressive and inclusive. For example, Christians could not be circumcised, thus effectively ending any conversions to Judaism and any proselytizing by Jewish people. If either Christians or Jews disobeyed, they would be exiled and their property confiscated. Christians and Jews could not intermarry, as this was officially considered fornication. The government impounded money sent to Palestine and to the Jewish people. The laws also barred Jews from public office. And, in many places throughout the empire, Jews were legally prohibited from celebrating the Sabbath or Passover.

This anti-Jewish attitude was not solely political; it was religious as well. John Chrysostom, a highly respected and very influential fourth-century church leader, and committed follower of Yeshua, wrote concerning the Jews:

> [They are] inveterate murderers, destroyers, men possessed by the devil. . . . Debauchery and drunkenness have given them the manners of the pig and the lusty goat. They know only one thing, to satisfy their gullets, get drunk, to kill and maim one another. . . . They have surpassed the ferocity of wild beasts, for they murder their offspring and immolate them to the devil. . . . They are capable of only evil. . . . Their synagogues may be likened to the abode of Satan. . . . Their souls are the abode of the devil. . . . The Jewish disease must be guarded against.

. . . Christians may never cease vengeance, and the Jew must live in servitude forever. God has always hated the Jews, and whoever has intercourse with the Jews will be rejected in the Judgment Day. It is the Christian's duty to hate the Jews. (*Homilies Against the Jews* 1:2–6; 6:1–6)

Augustine, the great church leader of the late fourth and early fifth century, asserted that the Jews have brought down on themselves divine judgment for all eternity. They must, therefore, forever be no more than mere slaves (Flannery 52–54).

These attitudes intensified during medieval times. The Crusades are a case in point. Their purpose was to free the "Holy Land" from the infidel invaders, the Moslems. Along the way, crusaders passed through many Jewish villages. A typical scene in these towns included rounding up the Jewish people, herding them into the synagogue, and then burning it to the ground with men, women, and children inside. This took place during the first crusade at the Great Synagogue in Jerusalem in 1099. Crusader armies eventually massacred tens of thousands of Jews on their marches to the "Holy Land."

Certainly, the plight of the Jewish people should have improved with the enlightenment brought about by the Scholastics. However, this was not to be. Witness the words of Thomas Aquinas:

The Jew is nothing more than an animal or servant. . . . It would be licit, according to custom, to hold Jews . . . in perpetual servitude, and therefore princes may regard their possessions as belonging to the state. (*Letter to the Duchess of Brabant*)

When the Black Death swept through Europe, India, and the Near East during the fourteenth century, the Jews were blamed. They were accused of poisoning Christian wells and of conspiring to "destroy the whole of Christendom." Fed by these rumors and accusations, religious mobs assaulted the Jewish quarters of towns and villages, dragged families from their homes, and burned them in bonfires.

The situation worsened during the years of the Inquisition. Forced baptism, confiscation of property, torture, and burning at the stake characterized this period for the Jewish people. Consequently, some 50,000 Jews died. The period culminated in 1492, with the sudden expulsion of the entire Spanish Empire's Jewish population, numbering about 300,000 people. The Spanish Jewish culture was one of the richest of its day. By this time, Jews had been living there peacefully for over four hundred years. They left Spain and her colonies, not realizing that starvation, enslavement, shipwreck, and death would face many of them before their hard journey was over.

One might expect the Reformation to ease the anti-Jewish attitudes, and in some measure, it did. However, virulent anti-Semitism continued—even in the writings of the Reformers. Luther, after previously being sympathetic to the Jewish people, charged them with being well-poisoners, ritual murderers, and parasites. In his venomous pamphlet, *Concerning the Jews and Their Lies*, he advocated their expulsion from Germany, along with the destruction of their synagogues, books, and writings.

> The Jews are brutes, their synagogues are pigsties; they ought to be burned. . . . They drag in the mire the divine words. . . . They live by evil and plunder; they are wicked beasts that ought to be driven out like mad dogs. . . . [Jews should] be forbidden on pain of death to praise God, to give thanks, to pray, or to teach publicly among us in our country. . . . They [should] be forbidden to utter the name of God within our hearing. (Luther 47:268–9)

Calvin did not do much better, calling Jews "profane, barking dogs, as stupid as cattle, a confounded rabble" (Calvin 25:665; 35:661; 40:605; 41:167; 50:307). Statements such as these, made by virtually all the Reformers, brought about the very actions suggested: the burning of synagogues, destruction of Jewish property, and the expulsion and death of Jews.

During the seventeenth century, religious Cossacks of the Ukraine and Little Russia massacred the Jews of Poland and the Ukraine for perceived ties to the nobility. In the span of ten years (1648–1658), over 100,000 Jews were killed by Cossacks, Russians, and Poles.

This was also the era of the rise and popularity of Passion Plays, the most famous being the performance at Oberammergau, which was first presented in 1634. Passion Plays portray the trial, crucifixion, and resurrection of Yeshua. These performances routinely, and quite emphatically, blamed the Jews—and only the Jews—for his death, portraying Pilate sympathetically and positively, a practice shared by most Easter sermons of the time. Eventually, these plays were performed throughout the world. They are still presented today. The hatred aroused by these Passion Plays, and stirred up by the Easter sermons, produced incredible violence against Jews in neighboring towns and villages, resulting in frequent Jewish deaths.

Moving into modern times, new forms of anti-Semitism developed while others continued. The early part of the twentieth century witnessed the appearance of *The Protocols of the Elders of Zion. The Protocols* claimed to provide evidence of a Jewish conspiracy, which was intent on conquering the world. It also fancifully asserted that Jews were the monetary powers behind, and the financial manipulators of, most nations and their governments. From these powerful positions, they set countries against each other to achieve their devious ends. A London correspondent exposed this vicious slander in 1921 as a fabrication of Czarist Russia and associated with the Russian Orthodox Church. *The Protocols* had been plagiarized from a French novel, and then combined with a German adventure story. Through the years, several thorough investigations, including one now part of the *Congressional Record* (August 1964), completely repudiated the *Protocols*. Unfortunately, the *Protocols* never received a proper burial, and have been repeatedly resurrected even in the twenty-first century, frequently in Moslem countries. The noted essayist and historian Hilaire Belloc was one of many who helped further the intent of *The Protocols*.

> We must not judge the Jews according to our ideas. . . . It is undeniable that every Jew betrays his employer. . . . The

> Jews cannot betray any country, for they do not possess
> one. . . . The Jew regards every country . . . as a place
> where he may find some profit for himself. (73, 210)

It is a sad fact of history that those who wrote—and those who
believed—these fabrications were intelligent, educated, and
usually religious men and women from "Christian" countries.

The Holocaust perpetrated by Hitler and Nazi Germany
looms as history's greatest anti-Jewish atrocity. Before it
ended, the Holocaust brutally exterminated over six million
Jewish men, women, and children—genocide beyond description, unparalleled in human history. Apart from some notable
exceptions, the virtual silence of the Christian community, and
in many cases its acquiescence or support, during these events
has shocked many thoughtful people. (See Goldhagen, *Hitler's
Willing Executioners*; Morse, *While Six Million Died*; Wyman,
The Abandonment of the Jews.)

More disturbing yet, as a study of *Mein Kampf* reveals,
Hitler viewed himself as fulfilling Luther's teaching concerning
the Jews.

> He believed himself to be the savior who would bring re-
> demption to the German people through the annihilation
> of the Jews, that people who embodied in his eyes, the sa-
> tanic hosts. When he wrote or spoke about his holy mis-
> sion, he used words . . . like "consecration," "salvation,"
> "redemption," "resurrection," "God's will." The murder
> of the Jews, in his fantasies, was commanded by divine
> providence and he was the chosen instrument for that task.
> He referred frequently to his "mission," but nowhere near
> so explicitly as in *Mein Kampf:* "Hence today I believe I
> am acting in accordance with the will of the Almighty Cre-
> ator: by defending myself against the Jew I am fighting for
> the work of the Lord." (Dawidowicz 219–20)

The teaching given elementary school students reflects
similar attitudes, as this quote from a third-grade text attests:
"Just as Jesus redeemed mankind from sin and hell, so did
Hitler rescue the German people from destruction" (Snoek vi).

In a Christmas speech in 1926, Hitler stated: "Christ was the greatest early fighter in the battle against the world enemy, the Jews. . . . The work Christ started but could not finish, I, Adolph Hitler, will conclude" (Wallechinsky and Wallace 452). Hitler further emphasized his connections with the church at a 1933 meeting with church officials. There, he declared that he "merely wanted to do more effectively what the church had attempted to accomplish for so long," maintaining that his actions were service to a common cause. In fact, the sign greeting Jews at Dachau, one of the most infamous of the Nazi death camps, read: "You are here because you killed our God." The buckles of SS soldiers often read: "God with us."

In Hungary, one day in 1944, a chaplain in full clerical garb appeared at the crowded Jewish hospital in Budapest and ordered all the patients into the courtyard. He held up a crucifix and shouted to the Hungarian Nazi Youth organization mob with him: "In the name of Jesus, shoot!" Only two Jews survived (Hajos 23). No wonder, quite often, Jewish people tend to view the Holocaust as another aspect of religious anti-Semitism.

The statements of Franz Delitzsch, an outstanding evangelical scholar of the past, accurately and graphically summarize the tragic history of contact between the church—both unbelievers and committed followers of Messiah—and the synagogue.

> The attitude of the Church to the Jews was almost willfully aimed to strengthen them in their antipathy to Christianity. The Church still owes the Jews the actual proof of Christianity's truth. Is it surprising that the Jewish people are such an insensitive and barren field for the Gospel? The Church itself has drenched it in blood and then heaped stones upon it. (*Allgemeine Evangelisch-Lutherische Kirchenzeitung*)

How could all of this have happened? How could a Jewish story be turned against Jews? When biblical passages were misinterpreted and the Gospels stripped of their Jewish setting, context, and content, their message was distorted. The result proved fatal to Jews.

The More Recent Story

The role of theological or religious attitudes makes up perhaps the most distressing aspect of anti-Semitism. These attitudes find expression in a number of statements: "God is through with the Jewish people"; "Jews are guilty of the death of Jesus"; "they were scattered and persecuted because they rejected Jesus"; "the Church has inherited all of Israel's promised blessings" (thus, effectively leaving only the biblical curses for the Jews). (For a biblical refutation of these positions, see Fischer, *The Olive Tree Connection*.) Sunday school materials subtly reflect similar sentiments by picturing Older Testament characters, Yeshua, and the apostles as European or Anglo-Saxon rather than Jewish, while the priests and Pharisees—those presented as opposing God—have stereotypical Jewish features.

A survey revealed the depths of anti-Jewish sentiment, even among theologically conservative churches. The survey found that 23% of liberal Protestants, 32% of Catholics, and 38% of conservative Protestants exhibited clear anti-Semitic attitudes (Selznik and Steinberg 108). Several examples reinforce these findings. In 1975, at one of the nation's leading Bible schools, posters announcing the meeting of a Jewish prayer group were covered over with Nazi swastikas (Fischer, *The Olive Tree Connection* 45). In 1976, a student at one of the country's foremost seminaries dogmatically asserted, "The Jews deserve everything that's been done to them, including the Holocaust" (Fischer, *The Olive Tree Connection* 45).

A recent study adds:

> There is abroad in our land a large measure of indifference to the most profound apprehensions of the Jewish people; a blandness and apathy in dealing with anti-Jewish behavior; a widespread incapacity or unwillingness to comprehend the necessity of the existence of Israel to Jewish safety and survival throughout the world. This is the heart of the new anti-Semitism. (Foster and Epstein 324)

Unfortunately, the appearance and popularity of *The Passion* has stirred the embers of anti-Semitism and reignited its flames. Surveys have already traced the results. According to the Pew Research Center poll released on April 2, 2004, the portion of Americans who blame Jews for the death of Yeshua has risen from 19% to 26%. The figure has more than tripled among those under the age of thirty, from 10% to 34% (*St. Petersburg Times*, "Survey Says Number of Americans Blaming Jews for Jesus' Death Rising"). Andrew Kohut, who directs the center and is one of the country's leading public opinion analysts, evaluated the results and ramifications of the survey.

> I don't think anybody could describe this finding as positive. . . . Our initial finding is that the belief that the Jews were responsible for the death of Christ is more prevalent than it was. . . . We found that this attitude is sharply higher among younger people who have seen the movie. (*St. Petersburg Times*, "Poll Finds Passion Strongly Sways Religious Perceptions")

While Kohut terms this result "puzzling," others might call it alarming.

No less shocking is the billboard unveiled on Ash Wednesday (Feb. 25, 2004), the same day the movie premiered. On its large outdoor marquee, located at a busy intersection in Denver, a Pentecostal church displayed the message: "Jews Killed the Lord Jesus. Settled!" ("'Jews Killed Jesus' Sign Causing Controversy!").

As if that were not enough, on February 22, 2004, at a very popular non-denominational fellowship on the eastern seaboard, the pastor delivered a blistering sermon, purportedly on Genesis 4. In it, he identified the Jews with Cain and Yeshua with Abel. He then emphatically declared: "Just as Cain murdered Abel, the Jews murdered Jesus Christ!" The vast majority of the several hundred congregants nodded in agreement.

A young Jew, destined to die in the Holocaust, poignantly describes the somber history explored in this chapter:

The Christians say they love him, but I think they hate him without knowing it. So they take the cross by the other end and make a sword out it and strike us with it! . . . Poor Jesus, if he came back to earth and saw that they had made a sword out of him and used it against his sisters and brothers, he'd be sad, he'd grieve forever. (Schwarz-Bart 364– 365)

And so, the distortion continues.

✿   ✿   ✿

For Further Reading

Bronner, Stephen. *A Rumor about the Jews.* Oxford UP.

Brown, Michael. *Our Hands Are Stained with Blood.* Destiny Image.

Carroll, James. *Constantine's Sword.* Houghton Mifflin Co.

Eckardt, A. Roy. *Elder and Younger Brothers.* Schocken Books.

Fischer, John. *The Olive Tree Connection.* InterVarsity Press.

Flannery, Edward. *The Anguish of the Jews.* Paulist Press.

Isaac, Jules. *The Teaching of Contempt.* Holt, Rinehart, and Winston.

Roth, John, and Berenbaum, Michael, eds. *Holocaust: Religious and Philosophical Implications.* Paragon House.

Ruether, Rosemary. *Faith and Fratricide.* Wipf and Stock.

Chapter 4

A Battle of Religious World Views

The release of *The Passion* and its accompanying publicity has created controversy in religious circles. Christians and Jews of various denominations and levels of scholarship have both criticized and praised the film. Reading through the reviews and interviews on all sides of the debate, it seems as though very different movies appeared on the screen, depending on the religious background of the viewer.

Each person in a film audience brings his or her "world view" with them when they see a film, just as each person brings their point-of-view with them when they read a novel or look at a work of art. A working definition of the term "world view" is the total knowledge, life experience, and emotional attitudes that a person has. Some disciplines use the term "schema" to describe the same collection of internal knowledge. This film shines a bright spotlight on the large gap between American Jewish and Christian world views. Responses to the movie have varied widely from person to person, based on whether they have a Jewish or Christian religious world view.

Your personal world view encompasses all the things you know to be true from your knowledge and experience. Usually, we do not consciously think about our world view. Yet, it accompanies us wherever we go and colors every decision we make. It embodies all of our prejudices and preconceptions, all our assumptions and stereotypes. However, our world view also contains "blank areas"—topics about which we have little knowledge, or indeed, no knowledge at all. If we're honest with ourselves, we can admit that we have no knowledge in a particular area. Sometimes, we think we know more than we actually do.

For example, if you have good hearing, you might try to imagine being deaf, in order to understand what life is like for those who are hearing-impaired. Hearing people, who have lived with the hearing-impaired, would be better able to describe the life of hearing-impaired people because their (hearing) world view has been broadened through actual observation and experience. To mix metaphors, they would be able to "see through another's eyes" what it is like to be deaf, having "walked in their shoes."

The only way to broaden our individual world views and incorporate other, more accurate, ideas is to gain knowledge and experience from those whose world view is different from ours. Most of us have neither the time nor inclination to run around looking for new and different world views to incorporate into our lives, but sometimes this is necessary.

The world views of American Christians and American Jews clearly conflict over the meaning and importance of the movie about the last day of Yeshua's life. A key to appreciating various world view issues is to understand that there are blank areas within both the Christian and Jewish world views. In other words, neither group has sufficient information about the other that would explain the other camp's "illogical"—in this context, meaning "not in keeping with *their* world views"—reaction.

Most people think that the world views of others are illogical, while their own makes perfect sense. When we say that Christians and Jews have different world views, by definition, we mean that they may not understand why people in the other camp get offended by something on a movie screen that seems perfectly logical to them. It may look like "the truth" to us, as "plain as the nose on your face," we might say.

As we go through a general list of facts that Christians and Jews often do not know about each other, we are not insinuating that people are inferior because they lack certain information. Nor, does a dearth of knowledge in these areas mean that a person is a bigot. On the contrary, to be ignorant of another's world view means there are blank spaces in knowledge and experience. It does *not* imply that a person is stupid or full of hate.

In America, Jews and Christians frequently "rub shoulders," socializing each day at work and in their neighborhoods. Yet, religion and politics are often seen as topics of conversation that are off-limits in polite society. It's time to discuss some of these taboo topics, thereby broadening our mutual world views.

What Many American Jews Do Not Know About Christians

Most Americans realize that Christianity is not one large amorphous mass of churches, but is divided into many branches and systems of church governance. For the purposes of discussing *The Passion of the Christ,* let's group Christians into the two largest types represented in the country: Protestants and Catholics (although this leaves out some specific denominations that are also important, like Orthodox Christianity). Not to be flippant or disrespectful, but the majority of Christians would express the primary distinction between the two groups like this: Roman Catholics belong to one big over-arching church that is run from Vatican City by their head bishop, the Pope. Protestants may be divided into large groups or denominations (Presbyterian, Lutheran, Baptist, Methodist), but an individual church may or may not answer to anyone higher in authority than the person who preaches the sermon every week. In fact, probably the most common answer a Protestant will give to an "outsider" about what it means to be a Protestant (as opposed to a Catholic) is "We don't believe in the authority of the Pope." Again, no offense is intended here, either to Protestants or Catholics. However, it is best to speak plainly about our world views. The sad truth is that not many Christians in America have thought about explaining these distinctions to non-Christians.

Protestants and Catholics do not have the same religious world view. In fact, they have *very* different world views. The differences appear in many areas, such as in the answers to the following questions: Who is in charge of individual churches? Which books are in the official Bible of your church? How do you conduct a typical Sunday worship service? Who can be a member of your church? Where do you go to find out what activities are permitted in your church? Do you consider members of other Christian churches "real" Christians? Do you have statues in your church? The Protestant answers to these questions and hundreds of others will be quite different from the Catholic answers.

What do Protestants and Catholics agree on? They agree on Newer Testament documents as the basis for all practice and faith. However, they would differ widely in the areas of Newer Testament (and Older Testament) interpretation and application. American Protestants often make this claim about their version of biblical interpretation, "We use *only* the Bible as our perfect guide, not the interpretations given by medieval saints or long-dead popes." Sometimes this concept is referred to as *sola Scriptura* (only Scripture), a phrase popularly used by Reformers (the earliest Protestants).

Many Protestants do not consider the Catholic Church to be authoritative (and vice versa, of course). The opinions of the Catholic Church do not impact their world view. Therefore, the question of whether the Pope or the Catholic Church as a whole approves of something (or not) is irrelevant to Protestants in the same way that the Dalai Lama's opinion is irrelevant. Later in our discussion, this insight will be important to remember.

When it comes to the topic of what Christians know about Yeshua's death, there is also a great disparity between the two camps. Catholics could be characterized as more-or-less experts on the Passion (the sufferings of Jesus in the period following the Last Supper, a Passover seder, and including the Crucifixion, as related in the Gospels) compared to most Protestants. The phrase "Passion of Christ" is not commonly used among Protestants.

A widely used part of preparation for the weekly Mass is a devotional exercise called the Stations of the Cross, which is regularly taught in the Roman Catholic Church. Each Station represents a specific moment in Yeshua's last day on earth.

There are fourteen Stations in this exercise, each of which has specific prayers associated with it. The purpose of these prayers is to focus the worshipper's attention on the sufferings of Yeshua for the sins of the world. This exercise is unknown and largely irrelevant to Protestant worship. It is worth noting that in *The Passion*, all fourteen Stations are portrayed in great detail. However, several of the Stations are not found in the Gospels, but are "additions" to the biblical accounts, probably inserted into Passion liturgy during the Middle Ages. Their appearance in the Gibson movie will be discussed later, in more detail.

What Many American Christians Do Not Know About Jews—and History

There seem to be just as many blank spots among Christians on the topic of Jewish faith and practice—perhaps even more. Because the vast majority of Americans regard themselves as Christians, they do not consider it relevant to learn anything about Jewish culture. Millions in our country do not have the opportunity to speak with Jews, much less have serious conversations on a regular basis. Although many Christians know that Yeshua, his family, and the apostles were Jewish, it is not relevant to their life and practice. Unfortunately, many Christians think they know about Jews and Judaism. However, their information is often based only on their knowledge of the Older and Newer Testaments, and the Jewish way of life as practiced in biblical times. This knowledge is sometimes spotty at best, and often not related at all to modern practices. Messianic Jews sometimes find it humorous to encounter Christians who tell us that they "met a Jew once." Then, the "enlightened" Christian proceeds to tell the Messianic Jews what the Jewish community is really like. Some Christians who have little contact with Jews may even base their perceptions of the Jewish people on popular personalities they see on television!

Generally speaking, the Jewish community in America is well-acquainted with the history of the relationship between synagogue and church. On the other hand, Christians are aware of very few specifics of the relationship. In synagogues, the history—both ancient and modern—of the Jewish people is a vital, ongoing topic, taught to every child and discussed in sermons and adult classes. Church history is rarely, if ever, taught formally in churches or parochial schools to any age group.

What's So Good about "Good Friday?"

Many in the American Jewish community understand a lesson from European Jewish history. Since the Middle Ages, the yearly presentation of Passion Plays fueled anti-Semitic attitudes. American Christians do not understand the direct connection between European Church history and their faith. Therefore, they cannot comprehend what their Jewish friends are so concerned about—the repetition in America of anti-Semitic acts of violence that inevitably followed performances of Passion Plays and Good Friday services in general.

Although not prominent in America, Passion Plays were a routine part of European Christian life. Even if a Christian did not go to see a Passion Play, Good Friday commemorations across Europe in Roman Catholic and Lutheran Churches were sufficient to send parishioners into the streets of Jewish neighborhoods, beating up Jews and burning their homes (Flannery 86–87, and see Judge). These events have been repeated for over 1000 years. They impact the way in which Jews perceive Christians. Millions of Americans who are originally from Europe, or their American-born children, still talk about these painful acts of persecution that resulted from distorted teachings within the church about the suffering and death of Yeshua. Today, most Christians do not have opportunities to hear their testimonies.

Golda Meir, former Prime Minister of Israel, was born in a Jewish village near Kiev, Ukraine. She stated that the first memory she had of a cross was seeing it being held aloft preceding a mob who came to burn down her town and terrorize and kill its citizens (qtd. in Fischer, *The Olive Tree Connection*

106). Her family was fortunate enough to immigrate to Milwaukee when she was a child.

[On a personal note, George and Marianne Fischer (our parents), who suffered through the Holocaust in Hungary as Messianic Jews, saw first-hand the results of the anti-Semitic teachings of Christian churches in Budapest.]

Many American Christians are ignorant of the connection between the Holocaust and the "Christian" nations in Europe. Since Americans were not directly responsible for perpetrating the Holocaust, they are often unaware of the direct links between Jewish persecution and Christianity. The Jewish community understands these links. A commonly heard explanation in America is that "genuine" or "born again" Christians would never hate or persecute Jews. Those who did so were merely Christians "in name only." As a wise professor once stated: "That's a distinction without a difference." To the average Jewish person, if the persecutor wasn't a Buddhist, Muslim, or Hindu, he was a Christian.

In the eyes of the Jewish community, Protestant and Catholic countries in Europe (those with official state churches) participated in the Holocaust. Jewish people see themselves as part of a global community of Jews. This "peoplehood" involves more than religious faith. On the other hand, Christians in the United States tend to be individualistic in their thinking. Their world view may be narrow; they only take responsibility for their own particular church or denomination.

The Potential for Prejudice

Scholars in several social sciences study how prejudice forms within people groups. Prejudice against other human beings is learned from other people; it is not God-given or biblically-based. Proponents of prejudice can take quotations from Scripture and thus "prove" that God does not approve of peoples of various colors of skin, or perhaps various nationalities. We are all aware that many Southern plantation owners in America, before the Civil War, considered themselves very fine Christians. They could point to many passages of Scripture to show that operating an American way of life based on slave labor was the way that God wanted the world to operate. In their world view, holding African-Americans as slaves was not only legal, it was good, and part of God's plan.

Why don't Americans consider slavery good anymore? Did the Scriptures change? By no means. Christian world views changed. Beginning in England, many stalwart Christians during the 1820s, such as the Earl of Shaftesbury and William Wilberforce, started to pry apart the supposed link between the Scriptures and slavery. Christians (lay people and clergy) spoke out, showing that slavery was unbiblical by arguing from the Scriptures that owning human beings and using them as property was wrong. Although slaves were owned during biblical times, slavery was neither God-ordained nor a good practice. The emphasis in *interpreting* the Scriptures changed, and that included recognizing the subhuman status of slaves in a system that had flourished in the United States since its founding. As this new interpretation of Scripture was taught throughout Christendom, the anti-slavery perspective became part of the Christian world view. "Slavery" became a dirty word, something that should no longer be connected with a "Christian" way of life.

Jews—a "Label of Primary Potency"

In just the same way, the Passion Plays, along with other liturgical works presented down through the centuries in Europe, labeled the Jews as "the enemies of God." In fact, the terms became almost interchangeable. If someone was a Jew, they were regularly seen as an enemy of the gospel. There were other commonplace thoughts in the European Christian world view about Jewish people—they were money-hungry, crafty, power-crazy, and loyal to no one outside of their own Jewish community. Each of these "truths" was emphasized yearly in every Passion Play and Holy Week liturgy. They influenced the world view of Christians. The word "Jew" became a dirty word.

Social scientists who study the nature of human prejudice call these sorts of descriptions "labels of primary potency." They are stereotypes so powerful that "they classify and block possible cross-classification" (O'Hara 160). These labels are so strong that using them in unusual ways creates oxymorons. Some examples will help. A "jock" is a label of primary potency applied to athletes. By labeling a person as a jock, you have said many things about him (although you could argue that there are female jocks). The stereotypical jock is dumb, muscle bound, and considers women as nothing more than sex objects. The terms "sensitive jock" or "insightful jock" are oxymorons, and if you wanted to say someone is a "smart jock," you would choose the term "academic all-American" instead. Other oxymorons that can be created using labels of primary potency are "freethinking bureaucrat," or "dainty feminist." Once a person has been identified with a label of primary potency, you cannot describe them with a broad range of individual human characteristics. They have been branded.

Not that all labels of primary potency are negative—they might be "positive." In a positive light, they merely assume attributes that "everybody knows" to be true. Nonetheless, they are stereotypes, which harm human relationships and block communication between groups. For example, many African-Americans may not dance well or like watermelon. In the same way, many Jewish people are not rich or extremely smart.

Stereotypes become harmful when they harden into labels of primary potency. A person who is stereotyped is no longer fully human in the eyes of the person doing the stereotyping. The stereotyping of Jewish people took place in European history during the Middle Ages with disastrous results. We will discuss this in the next chapter.

So, Why All the Passion about *The Passion*?

Jewish and Christian audiences bring their own world views with them when they see the movie—which was produced out of Mel Gibson's own world view (as producer, director, and scriptwriter, he had the final say). What the audience sees on the screen will confirm or conflict with their understanding of "how things were" during that fateful day in history. The audience will like the film and feel comfortable with its teachings if it conforms with their world view. The audience will dislike and feel uncomfortable about the film if it does not agree with its world view.

There is more than one acceptable opinion about any work of art. As the old proverb goes, "Beauty is in the eye of the beholder." Just because a viewer does not like *The Passion* does not mean he or she is "against the truth" or "against the gospel." They are simply watching the film through their own world view.

As Dennis Prager stated after seeing the movie:

> For two hours, Christians watch their Savior tortured and killed. For the same two hours, Jews watch Jews arrange the killing and torture of the Christians' savior. . . . Jews see Jews and Christians see Christians. (qtd. in Berman 1)

This result is what we should expect from a movie that aims at topics so hotly debated between these religious world views. The next chapter seeks to understand how Gibson was influenced by the distortion to produce such a controversial film.

✡ ✡ ✡

Chapter 5

A Modern Script for the Passion Story

Any consideration of a film should begin with the script. The script informs and directs the choices made in producing the film: the development of the characters and their dialogue, the sets, lighting, costumes, visual emphases, story-telling style, and editing. In a film which purportedly tells a true story about historical events, consideration of the "you are there" experience for the audience should be paramount. If a producer/director of a film wants to present a historically accurate rendition of the last hours of Yeshua's life, there are many fine sources from which to draw.

In this chapter, we will be examining the world view which influenced the production of the film *The Passion of the Christ*. This is crucial, not because anyone might consider Mel Gibson's world view wrong, distorted, or bigoted. Not because the film might be poorly crafted—because, on the contrary, it is *very* well crafted, using highly professional, modern film production techniques. We need to examine the world view that influenced this movie because Gibson's goal was to show what actually happened on that day.

A Very Catholic-Centered World View

Mel Gibson is a man who has strong religious convictions. As a member of a small branch of Catholicism called Traditional Catholicism, he holds in high esteem the traditional, older aspects of the Catholic faith—masses conducted in

Latin rather than English; the veneration of older ritual practices, as opposed to more modern rites. He does not keep his faith a secret; on the contrary, he talks about it when interviewed. Several of his starring roles have reflected his real-life faith in other contexts, most notably in *We Were Soldiers*, where he portrays a loving Catholic father who kneels in prayer with his children before leaving for an extended tour of duty in Vietnam.

It is understandable that any movie produced by Gibson about the life of Yeshua would be highly infused with his version of Catholic ideals. He combined forces with co-writer Benedict Fitzgerald to fill in the "gaps" in the gospel stories with details and incidents from several purely Catholic sources. He has openly named the sources as two nuns who experienced visions about the Passion stories, Sister Mary of Agreda (from Spain in the 1600s) and Sister Anne Emmerich (from Germany in the early 1800s). Their stories are based upon their lengthy visions, all of which are available in written form. It is not within the scope of this book to analyze their visions. We can say with confidence that each woman's visions are part of their world view and reflect their understanding of the Passion story. However, to the extent that their visions are interwoven with Newer Testament facts within the script, it is important to understand the nuns' impact on the movie that Gibson produced.

These two women are highly venerated by many people in the Roman Catholic Church. Their writings have been used many times by artists and sculptors in producing works of art based on various scenes from the Passion narratives. However, it is important to note that their writings may or may not have anything to do with what actually happened to Yeshua. They may not reflect what we know through archeology and historically verifiable written records to be true. Gibson insists that his movie presents Yeshua's death the way it actually was. It is important to consider this statement carefully. According to a study done by Beliefnet.com ("'The Passion': What's Not in the Bible?"), many incidents in *The Passion* are not found in the Gospels. A large percentage of them come from the writings of these two nuns.

Christian Theology—Good or Bad for Jewish People?

The two main divisions of Christianity in post-World War II Europe—Catholicism and Lutheranism—did some serious soul-searching after the war. It was hard to deny the evidence that the "Christian nations" in both Western and Eastern Europe had failed to educate their populace enough in Christian ethics to keep one-third of the Jewish population from the death camps. The negative view of Jewish people as portrayed in sermons, liturgy, and Passion Plays supported the vicious race hatred engendered by the Nazi Party throughout Christianized Europe. As a result, the Roman Catholic Church sponsored a self-study of their rituals, begun by Pope John XXIII and concluded under Pope Paul VI, which resulted in several reforms in 1965, now referred to as the Vatican II decisions. Lutherans were also involved in similar examinations of their own culpability for the Holocaust.

As part of its church-wide study, Vatican II examined the theology in its church rituals to see how Jewish people were portrayed to twentieth-century congregants. Their conclusion? They deeply regretted the picture of the Jewish people in the their catechisms. One of the most critical teachings was reformulated—that the Jews should not be held eternally responsible for the death of Jesus, as was formerly taught in Good Friday services and Passion Plays. In other words, the so-called "blood curse" on the Jews of Yeshua's time was cancelled by the words of Yeshua himself on the cross: "Father, forgive them, for they don't know what they're doing."

The blood libel statement by the relatively small group of Jews who gathered outside of Pilate's judgment seat on that fateful day 2000 years ago had been used as the excuse for persecution and even the murder of Jews. Down through the years, Christians were able to point to these words and say, "See, the Jews asked for it! They asked for this punishment from God. So they can't complain if it comes to them." However, Christian churches somehow failed to point out that the Savior they sought to "honor" had forgiven these very same Jews. The distorted interpretation of the Scriptures which had been preached for centuries was now going to be corrected.

Since Vatican II, Roman Catholic theologians and scholars have far outpaced any other Christian group in their active and ongoing historical investigation of Yeshua in his Second Temple setting. Important works by Raymond E. Brown and John Meier, among others, have brought the historical investigation of the Jewish backgrounds of Yeshua to the forefront of biblical scholarship. Other Catholic scholars, such as Edward Flannery, thoroughly investigated anti-Semitism's Christian roots and documented Christian complicity in persecution of Jews for hundreds of years. Jewish communities around the world continue to be encouraged by the type of books being produced by Catholic publishing houses. Quite a few joint Catholic-Jewish committees have met with the object of better communication and understanding between their groups.

The Passion Play Tradition

When drawing on sources to produce a script for his movie, Gibson and Fitzgerald could have called on the help and expertise of many of these great Catholic scholars and theologians. Instead, they drew on pre-Vatican II mystical stories and used them as primary sources for what Gibson termed "history," interweaving the visions together along with the texts of the Gospels. Traditional Catholics, of which Gibson is one, do not accept the Vatican II documents, or any other modern interpretations given by the papacy since the 1960s.

By calling his film, *The Passion of the Christ,* Gibson places his film in the long tradition of the Passion Plays. Passion Plays have been continuously performed in Europe since the Middle Ages (except in times of war), growing and expanding from the Medieval "mystery play" cycles performed as additions to the Catholic Mass. Passion Plays are primarily a European phenomenon, although they are still presented at several places in the United States such as Rapid City, South Dakota; Union City, New Jersey; and St. Augustine, Florida.

Traditionally, Passion Plays, as performed throughout Europe in the early Middle Ages, portrayed the entire last week of Yeshua's life, starting with the Palm Sunday processional into the city, and ending with his resurrection. After the 1200s, town guilds, outside the walls of the church proper, performed these plays, using townspeople as actors. The plays incorporated extra-biblical, entertaining, and even humorous scenes as part of the story. As early as the 1500s in Germany, they were performed entirely in German. Thus, they extended "church teachings" in a language-friendly format to semi-literate people whose worship services and educational system were entirely in Latin.

Passion Plays grew out of favor during the late 1700s, when the attitudes of the Enlightenment looked askance at the many superstitious scenes inserted into the gospel message. The sight of a devil in a red suit plunging a spear into Yeshua's side, accompanied by children dressed up as demonic imps, assisting him (among numerous other such scenes), were rightly viewed as embarrassing to the Christian faith. The Jewish leaders portrayed in these plays were caricatures of money-hungry, treacherous schemers, with black curly hair and hooked noses. On the other hand, Yeshua and the "good guys" had long straight hair and simple light-colored robes. The Ecclesiastical Council, headed by Maximilian Joseph, head duke of Bavaria, banned these plays in 1770 (Shapiro 66).

One town's version of the Passion Play has survived and prospered, even to this day: The famous Oberammergau Passion Play is still held in a small Bavarian town every ten years, and also on special occasions. It survives as a glimpse into the past, showing the way Passion Plays portrayed biblical events to literally millions of spectators down through the centuries. The history of the Oberammergau Passion Play has been recorded in many volumes written over the years, some even published by the town itself. The town council continues to exercise complete control over the play's production, including the script, casting, scenery, and outdoor theater. Its length is quite remarkable; the presentations usually last for about seven hours, including a lunch break.

Gibson's Film and Traditional Passion Plays

Except for its shorter length, Mel Gibson's movie follows in the footsteps of the medieval Passion Plays. The title of the movie itself advertises this link. In tenor, tone, and message, it is a modern-day presentation of traditional Passion Plays. Thematically, it has strong links to Passion Plays' distinctives and emphases. Although there is no outright acknowledgement by Gibson's movie of Oberammergau's influence, it is reflected on the screen in many ways. Just as there have been charges of anti-Semitism in Oberammergau's play by both Jews and Christians, that has also been true of Gibson's movie.

Because Gibson financed, produced, and distributed the film himself, he maintained control over the "vision" of the events of Yeshua's last day. No studio bosses asked him to change what he put on the screen. The popularity of the movie has been powerfully demonstrated by the enormous box office appeal it has had in America since its opening in February 2004. Gibson's filmed vision skillfully weaves together the historical documents of the Gospels, with the highly mystical stories of Catholic nuns to form his version of events. This linking has been so cleverly accomplished that even viewers well-versed in Newer Testament facts may not be able to trace where the gospel record stops and the nuns' stories begin.

Copies of scripts from both older and more modern versions of the Oberammergau production can be compared to Gibson's script. It would be extremely unlikely for there to be no similarity between the film and the Passion Play. After all, the words of all four gospels appear as the core of both the play and the film. Both the play and the film use the text of the four gospels, weaving the various events into one story.

Along with the testimony of the four gospels, both the play and the film include the Fourteen Stations of the Cross, although they are not overtly labeled as such. Once again, this should not be surprising since both the play and the film are strongly rooted in traditional Catholicism. Scenes in the film that are only found in the Stations of the Cross include Miryam's (Mary's) meeting of Yeshua while he is carrying his cross, and Veronica's kindness in offering Yeshua a cup of water, as he passes by her house. Protestant Christians who watch the film are probably unfamiliar with these scenes, but would accept their veracity in the same way as other scenes that would be part of the "poetic license" of the scriptwriters.

Both the film and the play use a "flashback" technique, whereby the forward flow of the story is interrupted by scenes happening at an earlier time. In Oberammergau, the story of Yeshua is interspersed with *tableaux vivants*—living diorama scenes from various parts of the Older Testament and the Apocrypha. There is no movement or dialogue in these scenes, which form a "living portrait" for the audience. A choir sings an extended chorale while the audience studies the tableau. These "still-lifes" are intended to focus the audience's attention on the suffering of Yeshua as prefigured by various characters from Israel's past, who also suffered rejection. Some of these *tableaux* include Joseph being sold into slavery by his brothers, Moses raising the serpent on a pole in order to save the Israelites in the wilderness, and others.

Gibson's film uses the flashback technique to give us previous action out of Yeshua's life, forming a backstory, or context, for the character of Yeshua. The storyline of the film starts in the Garden of Gethsemane, on Thursday night, and is completed in a little over two hours. Conversely, the current-day Passion Play starts its storyline with the Palm Sunday processional into Jerusalem, completing the actions of a week in about seven hours. The film shows us flashbacks such as the Last Supper and Palm Sunday, which are unnecessary in the live play. Other flashbacks highlight Miryam's viewpoint—including one of Yeshua as a toddler and a more extended scene of an adult Yeshua and Miryam.

The Catholic Milieu of *The Passion*

One of the most obviously Catholic emphases in the film is the deliberate spotlight on Miryam's role in the Passion story. She appears on screen more than the disciples, and she is at the center of several scenes as she follows Yeshua around Jerusalem. Peter refers to her as "Mother," an honorific term, not used in the Jewish community but very familiar to Catholics. It is not found in the gospel accounts. Yeshua's meeting with his mother as he is carrying his cross is one of the Fourteen Stations of the Cross. This is not corroborated by the Gospels. Miryam forms the visual centerpiece when Yeshua's body is taken down from the cross after the Crucifixion. The on-screen framing is an imitation of Michelangelo's famous sculpture, The Pieta (Italian: "pity"), of St. Peter's Cathedral, in Rome. The camera continually focuses on her suffering, thus portraying her in the role of co-redeemer, along with her son. In general, Protestants do not accept Miryam in this role, although Catholic and Orthodox Christians do. Gibson's church is well-known for their emphasis on Miryam's role in the redemption of humanity. This view of Miryam is very different from the Protestant view of biblical redemption. The film contributes to a portrait of Miryam as more than human.

Both Mary of Agreda's and Anne Emmerich's visions show Miryam in this pivotal role, quite different from the gospel accounts. Mary of Agreda's whole vision concerns Miryam's life and work. Anne Emmerich portrays her at the center of activity that day in Jerusalem, and also includes the storyline about Claudia, Pilate's wife. Claudia is not mentioned by name in the Gospels (but her name is supplied by Emmerich). She appears serene, dressed in white, to Miryam and Miryam of Magdala (Magdalene). She presents a stack of white linen cloths before Yeshua is flogged by the Romans. The two women then use the cloths to mop up Yeshua's blood from the stones by the flogging post. Later, they mop up more blood from the street. All of this activity is taken directly from Emmerich's account. Claudia, another example of a strong and noble woman like Miryam, plays an influential role in Yeshua's trial with Pilate. There, she tries to persuade Pilate to let Yeshua go free.

It is beyond the scope of this book to compare Emmerich's vision with Gibson's film point for point. There are at least a hundred overlaps, beyond the repetition of events explicitly stated the Gospels. Her influence is found throughout the entire film script and is reflected in the costuming, sets, and crowd scenes, contributing new characters and additional lines of dialogue. For the most part, Gibson's film is not merely about biblical events, but about Anne Emmerich's *interpretation* of biblical events. The bulk of her descriptions of Yeshua's last hours are now available in a modern film. Her world view, which obviously overlaps the filmmaker's, is that of a German nun from the 1820s.

Gibson's film is similar to Medieval Passion Plays in the way it connects Jewish people and money. In one of the first scenes in the film, the High Priest and his dark-robed cronies pay Judas thirty pieces of silver so that Judas will betray Yeshua to the Temple guards. The High Priest throws the bag of coins to Judas in the dark, underground room. Judas drops it, scattering the coins all over the stone floor. Judas immediately bends over and quickly scrapes up the coins on the ground. This scene has the potential to make Jewish people cringe. It is a visual representation of the slanderous notion that all Jews care about is money. It plays into this common anti-Jewish stereotype, and it is unnecessary to the flow of the story.

In the medieval Passion Plays, scenes (from early during Passion Week, a time not covered in Gibson's movie) told the audience a slanderous story that purportedly explained why Judas was a traitor. The Jewish money changers who had been thrown out of the Temple by Yeshua sought out Judas. The money changers knew that the High Priest and his cohorts wanted to get rid of Yeshua because he was too popular with the people. They wanted to trick Judas into turning against Yeshua in order to punish Yeshua for destroying their businesses. They succeeded in recruiting Judas to carry out their treacherous scheme, based on their love of money.

This anti-Semitic portrayal of Jewish people was included in Passion Plays and preached in sermons for hundreds of years, attempting the show that Jews loved money and would do anything for it, including putting an innocent man to death.

Another scene with this type of anti-Semitism comes directly from Emmerich's visions. She states that the High Priest's men went around Jerusalem giving money to Jews (presumably "bad Jews"), bribing them to go up to the Temple to testify falsely about Yeshua. In the film, a man in the black robes of the priests, knocks on a door and hands the inhabitant of the house a black bag. The inhabitant takes it. Once again, the film portrays Jews as manipulators of events because of their love of money.

Additional Scenes

Other scenes and characters in the movie were taken from the visions of Emmerich. One of the most notable is Satan's appearance in the Garden of Gethsemane. This scene is juxtaposed with the temptation in the Garden of Eden. Then later, in the same Garden scene, Yeshua crushes the head of a snake with his heel, a reference to Genesis 3:15, God's prophecy concerning the Messiah. This example of biblical imagery lends some weight to the film.

The Roman soldier who is redeemed also comes from Emmerich. In the gospel accounts, a nameless Roman soldier who is present at the crucifixion says "Truly this man was the Son of God." The movie provides this soldier with a backstory. It shows him being emotionally moved as Yeshua is led through the streets with the cross, the incident with Veronica, and finally his observation of the crucifixion itself. However, note the extra-biblical flourish at the end of his story—he becomes the soldier that pierces Yeshua's side to check to see if he is dead. The blood and water spurt out of Yeshua's side, hitting the soldier, causing him to fall to his knees. In traditional Passion Plays, the soldier who performed this act was called Longimus. He was blind. The blood and water which spurted out healed his blindness. Once again, this scene is not found in Scripture.

A Better Choice

Gibson could have used the work of any of the fine contemporary Roman Catholic scholars to inform his production. This would have made for a more historically accurate Passion Play. He could have taken the best of modern scholarship and archaeology to portray what is known about Second Temple Judaism. Instead of relying on Scripture exclusively, he chose to go to two "witnesses" who claimed they saw what "really" happened. In his mind, they were untainted by the effects of Vatican II and could be trusted not to modernize the sacred text.

Next, we will explore some specific cinematic choices Gibson made that demonstrate the influence of those who held distorted views of the gospel record. Specifically, we want to focus on the effects of these pre-Vatican II sources on the production of *The Passion*.

Chapter 6

Cinematic Choices That Could Lead to Anti-Semitic Conclusions

Several aspects of *The Passion of the Christ* are disturbing to those who have studied the history of Passion Plays and their effects on audiences through the ages. These plays do contain the actual words of Newer Testament Scripture. They do include the major people present at the events, and those present actually use the words found in Scripture. However, Passion Plays add events, people, and themes, which were not present at the historical event.

The Gospels do not describe the clothes of the characters, or where Yeshua's disciples actually were during the crucifixion (apart from Yochanan and Miryam of Magdala). They do not tell us what the Temple leaders looked like, in both demeanor and dress. The Newer Testament does not say how many people were in Pilate's courtyard, or what room Herod met Yeshua in. These details must be provided in any visual version of the story, however, and so must be "added" to the written text.

This challenge is not unique to this film. Filmmakers since the early 1900s have dealt with this period of history, and each has had to make the same kinds of decisions. These visual aspects also challenged the producers of Passion Plays. So, the current version of *The Passion* is probably no better, and certainly no worse, in its choices of visual and audio details.

Gibson's film is worthy of study precisely because it is in the same mold as traditional Passion Plays. It is not a new kind of Passion Play. Groups of Catholic and Jewish scholars have studied the different Passion Plays, sending pages upon pages of recommendations to the various producers in an attempt to get them to tone down the slanderous accusations against Jews. In the past fifty years, recommendations have been made to adapt these religious "set pieces" to reflect both the truth of the Gospels and a less hateful view of the Jewish people. For the most part, these scholars have been successful in their efforts.

Passion Plays have traditionally portrayed "the Jews" as enemies of Yeshua—and the "enemies of Yeshua" are the same as "the Jews." Even if it is made clear to the audience that Yeshua, Miryam, the disciples, Miryam of Magdala, Joseph of Arimathea, and all the common people who followed Yeshua were also Jews, it is equally obvious that these "good Jews" are different from the "bad Jews"—all of the Jewish leaders and the "crowds." This distorts the truth of the Gospels.

The townspeople of Oberammergau have been subject to constant scrutiny since World War II by both Catholic and Jewish groups. James Rudin, a leading American rabbi, who saw the 1984 production in person after reading and critiquing the written script as part of an American Jewish Committee group was "shocked":

> I realized that we had not missed the boat on the text, but that the costuming, the staging, the blocking were as important as the text. (qtd. in Shapiro 35)

In other words, it is possible to have the correct words in the dialogue and still spin the story with other visual clues. What visual clues do we have about the Jewish people in Mel Gibson's film?

The Costumes and Settings

The costumes of the Jewish people in the early parts of the film are very dark, almost monochromatic, in black and white. Historically, black clothes were not an option for many people during Yeshua's day—it was too difficult to dye clothes black with vegetable-based dyes. The least expensive clothing was made of linen or wool that would be left in its original shade of white or off-white. The clothing of wealthy Jews would be dyed with whatever colors were available. Consequently, when the chief priests are present at the crucifixion, they most likely would not be dressed in all black, as they are in the film. In fact, the costumes of the chief priests during that scene resemble *tallit*s (Jewish prayer shawls) that are black instead of their traditional white. There is no historic reason to do this other than to make a negative statement about these leaders.

Conversely, when Miryam and Miryam of Magdala appear in the early daylight hours out in the streets watching Yeshua, they both have a tight white head covering topped by a looser, black cloth, which flows down over their shoulders. These costumes distinctly portray them as nuns. They are not historically accurate costumes. The two women are approached by Shimon (Peter)—who, according to the Catholic world view, will become the first Pope. Shimon talks to them and addresses Miryam as "Mother." This is not a historically accurate title, and in the context of the black costuming, gives the strong impression that the group appears to be Catholic.

Another troubling aspect of the costuming is the decision to give the Jewish Temple guards very unusual headgear. Appearing in the very early scenes of the film, they arrive at the Garden of Gethsemane to arrest Yeshua, led by Judas. They do not wear metal helmets (as the Roman soldiers do later on) but have—what appear in the dim light to be—hats made out of leather strips. This seems like a historically acceptable alternative to metal helmets, except for the additions to the top of the leather strips—groupings of miniature spikes sticking out of their headpieces. An enlarged version of one of these spikes will appear in the crucifixion scene, as it is pounded into Yeshua's hands and feet. What is the purpose of this historically inaccurate and unusual costuming effect? Is its purpose to foreshadow a future event? These guards, about whom we know very little, appear to be quite gruesome characters. They certainly operated under the strict watchfulness of the Roman authorities. In any case, they are also Jews, like Miryam and Shimon, and Yeshua himself. But, when appearing as "bad Jews" in Gibson's film, they wear these strange headpieces.

The film was shot in Italy on sets or in actual buildings that appear amazingly authentic. The Mediterranean sunshine and the dusty dirt of the road to Calvary look very much like what you might find in modern-day Jerusalem. However, the inner rooms of the Temple, with their bare rough-hewn walls and poor lighting show little of the expansiveness and majesty of Herod's Temple. The deliberations of Caiaphas, Annas, and the other priestly leaders did take place at night. However, in the film, the men seemed disorderly and cramped in small, dimly lit rooms. It seems more like the gathering of a vigilante mob than a formal meeting of established leaders and friends of Rome that they were.

Additionally, they are not seated at any point during their deliberations—not when they meet with Judas, not when Yeshua is brought before the High Priest. There is no furniture in any of the rooms where Jewish leaders are seen. They appear to be standing in big, empty stone rooms with low ceilings. Why is there always a group of such high-ranking officials swarming around in the dark? Wouldn't they have used servants or messengers to accomplish their goals while they remained in the relative comfort of the majestic Temple? Are the Jewish leaders shown this way to portray them as manipulative and meddling—through money and treachery, doing their best to assassinate Yeshua?

The Jews As a Big, Angry Mob

Throughout the movie, most of the Jewish population seems to be on the edge of hysteria or mob rule. This is in stark contrast with the aforementioned "good Jews," who remain strong, noble, and heroic, suffering in relative silence. This interpretation of the Passion story comes straight out of both the traditional Passion Plays and the writings of Anne Emmerich. Her vision continually portrays Jews yelling, screaming, tearing their clothes, and storming through the streets like a lynch mob. Yeshua's garments are stripped off and replaced by others on at least five occasions, each time with more taunting, rock throwing, and spitting from those around him. The crowd seems uncontrollable in its rage and perhaps mentally unbalanced, given the calm and quiet demeanor of Yeshua.

In the film, Satan (herself) appears at intervals, peeking out from behind the screaming mobs. Ironically, the very image that those of the Enlightenment wanted eliminated from the public eye is one that has been restored to this modern Passion Play. In one scene, this satanic woman, an original character in the Gibson film, carries a baby who sits up, revealing a demonic face. This may be a representation of an "anti-Madonna," and as such, can be accepted by the audience as poetic license. She does not appear in Emmerich's visions, but Satan himself does.

Also restored to the modern version from traditional Passion Plays are demonic children who are shown, without explanation, hounding Judas to his death (as if they are necessary for Judas to decide to commit suicide). They are taken directly from Emmerich's visions. The film makes it clear that Satan is at work in the events of Yeshua's final day. However, doesn't this portrayal hide the fact that Yeshua willingly chose to die? If Satan is theoretically orchestrating his death behind the scenes, then God is not in control of the situation. Who *is* in charge here? It is not clear, because these scenes need to be interpreted to the audience by the filmmaker. They are not. Perhaps Gibson is implying that as their meaning is so obvious, no explanation is required.

As Yeshua is led through the streets after his death sentence, the Jewish crowds are angry and hostile. Men and women are yelling, pumping their arms in the air, and throwing stones at Yeshua, as he walks by. Their angry voices echo off the stone walls of the city. Yeshua falls down in this hostile territory, and is met by his mother. When he is forced to rise again by the cruel Roman soldiers, within the space of about fifty feet, we see no more angry Jewish people. Instead, the Jewish people are sad. Where did all the angry people go in such a short time?

This is a good example of the mistakenly depicted, angry, bloodthirsty mobs of the Passion Plays. Emmerich portrays the Jewish leaders in Jerusalem as rich, insensitive taskmasters, who are cruel to the poor tradesmen, who gladly follow Yeshua. She presents this downtrodden group as "good Jews," who are at odds with the evil leadership. Then, she shows us a close-up view of these poor downtrodden people, whom she has identified as followers of Yeshua. They consist of an inordinate number of women who appear to be Roman Catholic. Clearly, Emmerich's vision is centered in her personal 1820s German world view.

The degree of torture, blood, violence, and gore portrayed in the film overshadow the fact of Yeshua's willingness–and plan—to die. Repeatedly, with alarming detail, the audience is shown how cruel human beings can be. These intense scenes, and more, appear in visions of Emmerich. In them, Miryam swoons or faints about fifteen times. Miryam of Magdala swoons and screeches in anguish, throwing herself repeatedly at Yeshua's feet. Yochanan helps the women to keep going. He is the only male follower shown, one who never speaks (Emmerich's description says that he was silent.)

The long scenes of scourgings are not found in the Newer Testament documents. There, the description of Yeshua's torment appears in one sentence (Matt. 27:26; John 19:1). The close-ups of Yeshua being whipped, repeatedly, on both sides of his body are meant to focus the audience on his suffering. Interestingly, famous woodcarvings from the Middle Ages, which are used as altarpieces in several German Catholic Churches, show bloody wounds over every inch of Yeshua's body. Modern historical research reveals the scourgings only took place on the victim's back.

Pilate, the Voice of Reason

This melodrama highlights the disparity between the Romans—stoic and calm—and the Jews—hysterical and anguished. Viewers of *The Passion* have noted that Pilate does not seem like such a fiend. This is in direct contrast to the way contemporary authors depict him. Indeed, he was a cruel and manipulative man who ruled with an iron fist. The movie shows him living with his wife in his palace, but in reality, they did not live in Jerusalem. Pilate's seat of power was in Caesarea, so presumably, they were visiting Jerusalem. The rooms that

Pilate and his wife Claudia (her name does not appear in the Newer Testament, but again, Emmerich supplies this) walk in and out of are full of light-filled windows, gauzy curtains, and breezes.

In the film, Claudia appears sweet and regal in her white robes. This image is lifted straight from Emmerich's vision, along with the kind gift of white linen cloths to Miryam. Later in Emmerich's story, Claudia becomes quite distraught when her husband is "unable" to save Yeshua's life. Running away from Pilate later that weekend, she becomes a Christian. Eventually, she accompanies Rav Shaul on his voyages—a fact not supported by the Newer Testament.

Pilate is pictured as the true nobleman, civilized and calm, intent on keeping his job as the Roman procurator over the money-hungry, cruel Jews. His wife approaches him, with a warning about not killing an innocent man she has seen in her dreams. Consistently, Pilate appears as a gentleman. In contrast with the angry and unruly Jewish mob he must try to control, he speaks to Yeshua in a reasonable tone, offering him a glass of water. To satisfy the crowd's bloodlust, he has the Roman guards flog Yeshua. However, this is not enough punishment to satisfy the mob, so insistent are they that Yeshua must die. Pilate offers to release a criminal to them in honor of Passover, but they opt to free Barabbas (a murderer with ugly teeth whom they all despise) instead. There is no satisfying the crowd.

Though Pilate finds Yeshua innocent, he feels trapped. The mob threatens to tell Caesar that Pilate is going to let a known insurrectionist go free. The meddling, unreasonable Jews have forced him to do something that he would not normally do— to keep his job, and possibly his life. Reluctantly, he sentences Yeshua to death by crucifixion, ordering his soldiers to carry out the judgment.

This is the portrait of Pilate found in the Passion Plays, and expanded upon in Sister Emmerich's visions. The audience can identify with him, a person caught between the proverbial rock and hard place, between the wrath of the Jewish mob and the anger of Caesar. Ironically, Hitler identified with this portrait of Pilate when he saw the Oberammergau Passion Play during its 300th anniversary season, in 1934. Later, when discussing the Passion Play at a dinner party, Hitler was recorded as saying:

> It is vital that the Passion Play be continued at Oberammergau; for never has the menace of Jewry been so convincingly portrayed as in this presentation of what happened in the times of the Romans. There one sees in Pontius Pilate a Roman racially and intellectually so superior, that he stands out like a firm, clean rock in the middle of the whole muck and mire of Jewry. (qtd. in Shapiro 168)

Unfortunately, Gibson's portrait of Pilate seems to be far more similar to the "firm, clean rock" than the tyrannical Pilate of history.

The Issue of the Skullcaps

Whether Jewish men of this time wore skullcaps (*kippot* or *yarmulkes*) is a matter of some debate. Artistic decisions made should be made with consistency. This was not the case in *The Passion of the Christ*. The costume director, under Gibson's direction, showed the "bad Jews" that is, those who were Yeshua's enemies, wearing skullcaps. The "good Jews," Yeshua and his followers, did not have their heads covered. Gibson was making a statement through his costuming choices.

Interestingly, Simon of Cyrene—who was forced by the angry mob to carry Yeshua's cross (and not too happy about it)—was initially wearing a skullcap. After bearing the cross for a time, and suffering abuse similar to Yeshua, he softens up. During the last scene in which we see him, he is portrayed as someone who might be considered a new follower of Yeshua. As he walks away from the camera, he is no longer wearing a skullcap. Though this may be a continuity mistake—the film equivalent of a typographical error—considering the ambiguity about skullcaps in the movie, it is unlikely. Most probably, it is another costuming decision, a statement by Gibson.

The Coup de Grace

Most audiences may barely notice the most slanderous, anti-Semitic scene in the movie. It contains neither blood nor whippings. In fact, no pain of any kind is inflicted, at least not the kind of suffering that Yeshua experiences for almost two hours. This scene probably lasts no more than thirty seconds—yet, its impact is very powerful.

At the moment of Yeshua's death, earthquakes and thunder rumble through Jerusalem. This is vividly portrayed in the film. People leave the area of Calvary fearfully. As the wind picks up, they are seen heading off toward their homes within the city walls. For a brief moment, we see a room constructed with charcoal gray stone walls. A throne-like object is in the background, and a chiffon-like "curtain" (about the size of a large woman's scarf) is ripped in two from the top down. The floor rises and splits down the middle as though a large zipper is being unzipped. At the far end of the hall, the camera reveals that the throne-shaped, stone-like bench has been broken in half by this earthquake at the exact moment of Yeshua's death.

This scene could be interpreted to represent the end of the Jewish faith. Presumably, the room is the Holy-of-Holies, in the Temple, although no explanation is offered. The curtain is representative of the tapestry that covers the Most Holy Place, in the most holy Jewish site. The Gospels do confirm that the veil was torn from top to bottom at that moment (Mark 15:38; Luke 23:45), an event the Talmud refers to as well (*Yoma* 39b), although the connection with Yeshua's death is not mentioned there. In the film, the rest of the destruction of the Temple comes from Emmerich's visions. She also envisages large parts of Jerusalem turned into rubble, people running through the streets in panic. The stone-like bench, representing the Mercy Seat, is broken. The room is empty—no people are present, and certainly no *Shekhinah* (the glorious visible expression of the invisible God of Israel). All is gone. The implication is that Judaism is finished.

This very dramatic scene depicts a distortion of the truth. In reality, the Temple in Jerusalem continued to be the center of

Jewish sacrifice and worship for another forty years, until the Roman legions destroyed it in 70 C.E. The disciples of Yeshua continued to worship there, teaching in its courtyards. New believers in Yeshua went through the *mikvah* (baptism) in ritual pools underneath the Temple steps. Rav Shaul continued to worship there and keep the Temple traditions (Acts 21:20–26).

Judaism does not die on the cross—the Jewish Messiah does. The Temple does not fall in retribution for the death of Yeshua. The Jewish people are not punished for the death of the Jewish Messiah. At the moment of his death, Yeshua asks his heavenly father to forgive them, saying "they don't understand what they are doing" (Luke 23:34). If the God of Israel did not answer that prayer, then God will not answer *anyone's* prayers.

This important fact seems to have been overlooked by Mel Gibson, revealing the world view of the script writers and of Emmerich. They portray the Jewish religion as being destroyed by God on that day—to be replaced by "good Jews," Gentiles, and Yeshua. This view leads to anti-Semitism—and ultimately —led to the Holocaust. The Roman Catholic and Lutheran Churches both acknowledged this after World War II (see Gerlash and Barnett, and Phayer).

Our goal has not been to denigrate Mel Gibson personally. We merely want to point out that some of his cinematic choices were informed by more than the gospel. He allowed distortions—passed down through the Passion Plays and promulgated by the visions of Anne Emmerich—to influence the content of his film. People need to be aware of this fact.

In the next chapter, we set the record straight by explaining God's master plan for humanity. He chose the Jewish people, through whom to bring the Messiah and bless the world. It's time for 2000 years of misrepresentation to come to an end.

✿ ✿ ✿

Chapter 7

God's Master Plan for Humanity

Most people realize that the Romans actually killed Yeshua. Nevertheless, many people forget that Yeshua's death was the core of God's plan for restoring his world. Others are uninformed, or simply do not understand God's purposes.

This very Jewish story begins in the first book of the Torah, Genesis. As part of his commitment to restore all of creation, God promises Adam and Eve that her "seed would crush the head of the serpent" (Gen. 3:15). Not only is the structure of this text intriguing, its choice of words is fascinating. The passage begins with hostility between Eve and the serpent and their respective "descendents." But then, in a surprise move, it shifts dramatically to focus on an individual descendent ("he") among Eve's "seed," who will conquer, not the "seed" of Satan, but the serpent himself! The Hebrew word to describe Eve's "seed" (*zera*) is quite unexpected. It is a term usually reserved for males in biblical and rabbinic literature, and in modern Hebrew refers to male semen. The text clearly hints at a very unusual birth, a story picked up in Isaiah 7:14 and the Messiah's promised "virgin birth." The promise also alludes to the death of Eve's special seed ("bruise his heel"), and, most importantly, the verse reminds us that God will bring all this about ("I will cause . . . "); it is his plan for the ages. The ancient rabbis understood the significance of Genesis 3:15 when they asked: "This is the seed that is coming from another place. And, who is this? This is the king Messiah" (*Bereshit Rabba* 51).

Another cryptic but significant passage found in the Torah is Numbers 24:17, part of Balaam's prophecy about Israel: "A star will step forth from Ya'akov [Jacob], and a scepter will arise from Isra'el." The rabbis of the Talmud (*J. Taanit* iv. 8), Rabbi Akiva, and the Ramban (Rabbi Nachmanides) all identify the "star" as the Messiah. He would rule and enact God's purpose for earth.

God's Plan for the Ages Unfolds–The Abrahamic Contract

To appreciate God's program for his world, it is vital to understand God's purposes for the Jewish people. The Torah contains the outline of that plan. As part of this, Genesis 1–11 is striking. It condenses numerous happenings over a long period into several chapters. For example, these chapters say little about such outstanding events as the creation and the flood, events about which many want to know more. God seems to say, "This is not the main point; these are not the most important things for you to know." He rushes through these events to something more significant, something found in chapter 12. Chapters 1–11 cover a long, indeterminate period, whereas chapters 12–50 cover less than two hundred years! So, the structure of Genesis clearly indicates that God definitely emphasizes this latter section of the book, and chapter 12 stands as the turning point.

In this chapter, God chooses Abraham and makes several important promises to him. These pledges contain, in seed form, the basics of God's purpose for the world. The promises, and their later expansions, are often called the Abrahamic Covenant or Contract. By understanding the terms of the contract, we can better understand God's actions through the rest of Scripture and in the history of the world—past, present and future. Verses 1–7 contain three key terms which unlock God's purpose: land (vv. 1, 7); nation, or its synonym, seed (v. 2); and blessing (vv. 2–3). God promises to give Abraham and his descendants the land of Canaan. He promises to multiply them and make them a great nation. Finally, God promises to make them his instrument for blessing the world. He then describes these promises in three ways.

Genesis 13:14–18 contains the first two ways. In verse 15, God says to Abraham, "All the land which you see I will give to you and your descendants forever" (cp. 17:7–8). The text clearly states that God's contract with Abraham is a "forever" contract; it is eternal. The second way God describes the contract arises from verses 14–17. God tells Abraham to look around at the land he would give him, and then to walk through it. The land Abraham saw, the ground he walked on, was real land, a definite, concrete, tangible piece of geography. God was *not* using metaphorical or symbolic language.

In chapter 15:3–5, God tells Abraham that his seed (descendents) would originate from his own body and then multiply greatly. His seed also would not be something merely metaphorical or symbolic; they would be real, physical children and grandchildren descended directly from him. Consequently, Abraham expected a real piece of geography and descendents coming from his own body. So, God's promises to Abraham were literal, not symbolic.

The third important way God describes the contract is found in chapter 15:7–18. God instructs Abraham to prepare the items used in ratifying Near Eastern contracts at that time. Animals are taken, cut in half, and separated. The contracting parties would then walk between the halves to ratify the agreement. So, Abraham thought he and God would do this. However, verses 17–18 show that only God walked between the halves, not Abraham. By doing this, God indicated that he alone was responsible for the terms of the contract. The contract's fulfillment depended on him, not Abraham. It was not conditioned on Abraham's follow-through or his descendants' actions. It was unconditional and unilateral, depending solely on God's promise and commitment to carry it out (see Gal. 3:17–18).

So, the Abrahamic Contract includes the land, a seed, and great blessing; and the Bible describes these promises as eternal, literal, and unconditional. God then confirms the contract with Abraham's son, Isaac (Gen. 17:19), and later with Isaac's son, Jacob, and his descendants (Gen. 28:13–14). Jacob's descendants became the Nation of Israel, the Jewish people. The

Land of Canaan, which God gave to Abraham and the Jewish people has been known historically as Israel, or at times, Palestine. (Its borders are described in Genesis 15:18). The Abrahamic Contract, then, guarantees the permanent national existence of the Jewish people, their perpetual title to the Land of Israel, and the certainty of God's blessing on them, and ultimately on the whole world through them. The rest of Scripture and history unfolds this contract and shows how God works out his purpose for his world.

God had promised to create a Nation out of Abraham. Several things were essential for this: a people, a government, and a homeland. Genesis 12–24 relates the story of the man God chose, Abraham. In chapters 25 to 45, God selects the people, i.e., which of Abraham's descendants he would work through, and then tells the story of their lives. He specifies the promised line of Abraham as going through Isaac and Jacob. Genesis 46 to Exodus 18 recounts how God preserved the people he chose. In Egypt, the family multiplied sufficiently to become a nation (about two million people left Egypt with Moses). God miraculously preserved them through the Egyptian oppression and their wanderings in the desert.

A Nation in Its Land—The Mosaic Contract

God had provided the first essential for nationhood, a people. When the people arrived at Mount Sinai, he gave them the second essential. God provided a constitution for the Nation (Exod. 19 to Lev. 27, and the entire book of Deuteronomy), thus establishing its government. This was the covenant communicated through Moses.

The literary structure of the Mosaic covenant resembled that of the international treaties of the time. It was in the form of a treaty between a servant nation and a great king. God, the great King, graciously specified for Israel, the servant nation, the conditions for living under his rule. These explained the details of living the totality of their lives before him. Since God was sovereign over every area of life, there could be no distinction between sacred and secular. This was a true theocracy. Therefore, its constitution contained principles for conducting governmental as well as social, family, and personal affairs; principles for maintaining and expressing a proper relationship with God (not of entering such a relationship, which they had already done through the Exodus)—although surrounded by a godless society; and promises and warnings concerning their stay in the land.

God expected Israel to be a kingdom of priests (Ex. 19:5–6), acting as a "lighthouse" bringing others to himself. To do this, they had to be holy, which means "set apart" or "distinct." This kind of holiness comes when people obey God. So, the people of Israel were to live God's way, and then others would be attracted to him by their distinctiveness (Deut. 4:5–10).

God promised that if the people kept the guidelines of the Mosaic Contract, they would experience his blessings, be a blessing to others, fulfill their calling, and enjoy life in the Land. However, if they did not, the results would be automatic (Deut. 11:26–28). Deuteronomy mentions these blessings and results. Chapter 28 predicts Israel's disobedience and the ensuing discipline of God, which culminated in their dispersion. In chapter 30, God then promises to bring them back to the Land of Israel as part of their restoration to him. It is all part of God's covenant-commitment love (Hebrew: *hesed*) for his people.

The contract tells the people how to live properly before God so they can enjoy life in the Land and what will happen if they do not. It also explains God's subsequent program for the Jewish people with respect to the Land. Therefore, the Mosaic Contract expands the Abrahamic Contract's Land promises.

After receiving their constitution and government, the only essential remaining for nationhood was the possession of the homeland. The book of Joshua records God's giving Israel the Land he promised. God had now completed his creation of a Nation. He had prepared it both to be and to receive a blessing.

Next, Israel moves into the time of the judges (Judg. 1 to 1 Sam. 11). Anarchy and turning from God characterized this period. People "did their own thing," whatever they felt was right (Judg. 21:25). They forgot about God and what he had done (Judg. 2:1ff.). The result, as God had warned them in Deuteronomy, was oppression from outside and corruption inside the Nation. Even when he raised up judges to liberate them and the people finally turned back to God, they quickly turned away again. At the end of this period, they asked for a king, and God granted their request.

Inconsistency characterized the time of the kings (1 Sam. 12 to Zeph. 3, excluding Ezra, Nehemiah, Esther, Ezekiel, and Daniel). The king's leadership and example were crucial. If he remained faithful to God, the Nation worshiped and obeyed God. If the king turned away from God, the Nation did too. Unfortunately, most kings turned their backs on God and led Israel down a miserable road. However, David came closest to being an ideal king; it was with him that God ratified another important contract.

The Promised Seed—The Davidic Contract

The primary passages dealing with this contract are 2 Samuel 7:5–16 and Psalm 89:1–37. They expand the Abrahamic Contract's seed promises. In fact, the Davidic Contract describes Abraham's greatest seed, the Messiah, as the one who will reign over the earth with Israel—the rest of Abraham's seed—as the center of his rule.

David wanted to build a "house" (Temple) for God. God refused to allow this and used the occasion to make great promises to David. Some of these concerned David's son Solomon, who would build a "house" for God. Others went far beyond Solomon. God promised to build an eternal "house" for David. Near Eastern cultures often used the image of a house to indicate a line of descendants. So here, God guarantees that David's line (or seed) will never be completely wiped out.

Next, he promised to establish David's throne forever. A throne signifies the authority to rule. In other words, the authority to rule Israel would always belong to David and his descendants. His family would never be displaced by another as the rightful royal line. God also guaranteed the existence of David's kingdom forever. The word "kingdom" implies a domain, the physical place of a reign over existing people. Hence, God promises that a kingdom will always exist over which David's line will rule, a kingdom that will have Israel at its center. Thus, the Davidic Contract, like the contracts before it, guarantees Israel's ultimate, continued existence.

However, there was a condition attached to part of the contract. Disobedience on the part of David's descendants would result in God's judgment (2 Sam 7:14–15; Ps 89:30–34); the disobedient individuals would not participate in the promised blessings. They might also lose their part in ruling Israel. They would not experience the blessings because they would not appropriate them by faith. Yet, disobedience would not invalidate the covenant (Ps. 89:30–34). David's seed would remain the royal line. Changing forms of government, or divine judgment, might interrupt the actual rule over the kingdom by David's line. However, the line, the right to the throne, and the royal domain would be preserved and never lost—despite sin, captivity, intrigue, or dispersion. The attempt by Queen Athaliah to exterminate the royal line and the survival of Joash (2 Kings 11) provides a good example of God's preservation of David's royal line.

Therefore, continuous political government did not need to exist, but the line with its rights had to be preserved and ultimately restored. Thus, the Messiah's rule over Israel on David's throne is founded on the Davidic Contract. And, based on this contract, the prophets expected Messiah, as David's greatest descendent and Abraham's promised seed, to restore David's kingdom and reign over Israel in millennial blessings (Jer. 23:5–6). David's line was preserved and eventually culminated in the Messiah. It will yet be restored in all its fullness.

The prophets (Isaiah to Malachi) functioned during the time of the kings and afterward. Often, they acted as prosecuting attorneys, i.e., they indicted the Nation for its disobedience. Their books read almost like courtroom scenes. They also preached the covenants. The Mosaic Covenant had promised blessings for obedience and judgment for disobedience, so the prophets had nothing but judgment to offer the Nation for their disobedience. Yet, their message ends with hope because the Abrahamic and Davidic Covenants promised that God would use Israel to bless the world and be the center of Messiah's reign. As the prophets surveyed the situation, this was not happening. But God had promised that this would be a reality. Therefore, it still had to happen, and they looked forward to this time. As part of this anticipation, and through the context of the prophets, God revealed the "New" Covenant.

The Culmination of the Blessing Program—The "New" Contract

The "New" Contract (Jer. 31:30–39; 33:14–22; Ezek 36:22–32) expands the Abrahamic Contract's blessing promises, and shows how Israel will be a source of blessing for the entire world.

The contract's terms, made specifically with Israel (Jer. 30:31), are spiritually radical. God promises to wipe out sin. He promises to give his people a new nature with new drives to obey him and keep his guidelines. And, he promises to put his Spirit in his people to energize their new nature. He promises to establish an even more intimate relationship with his people, and eventually with all humanity. Ultimately, these tremendous blessings relate to Israel's restoration and the worldwide benefits of Messiah's reign (Jer. 31:37–39). At that time, the entire earth will share in this blessing. However, individuals can enter into many of these blessings today by responding to God (Ezek. 36:25–27; see also John 3:5, 7, 10).

The specific Hebrew and Greek words for "new" (*hadash* and *kainos*) can mean "renewed." They are often used to describe the process of renewal (for example, the renewal or recurrence of the moon's cycles, or the refurbishing of a house). The terms and structure of this covenant also imply a renewal and ratification of the existing contracts (Jer. 33:14–22).

Yeshua identified himself as the "Renewed" Covenant's mediator or ratifier (Matt. 26:28; Luke 22:19–20; Heb. 9:15).

He made it possible for it to go into effect and for people to enjoy its benefits. The dynamic coming of the Holy Spirit at *Shavuot* (Pentecost), then, signaled the Renewed Contract's initiation. At that time, God indicated that he had dramatically put his Spirit in his people, as promised in the terms of the contract (Ezek. 36:24–27). Its other terms, as well as the unfulfilled promises of the other covenants, await a future fulfillment.

The Older Testament's last statements (Mal. 3:22–24, or 4:4–6) underline the centrality of these contracts. The prophet tells God's people to follow the Mosaic Covenant's guidelines, as the way of life that pleases God. He then alerts them to look for the coming of Elijah, the forerunner of Messiah, the Messiah who fulfills the Abrahamic, Mosaic, and Davidic Contracts, and institutes the Contract of Renewal.

The Newer Testament carries on the flow of the covenants. Mattityahu, for example, introduces Yeshua as the son of Abraham and David (Matt. 1:1), a theme he follows throughout this gospel to show that Yeshua fulfilled these contracts. In the Sermon on the Mount, Yeshua presents himself as the Mosaic Covenant's fulfillment as well (Matt. 5:17). Before Yeshua's birth, the angel who visited Miryam announced that the child would be given his father David's throne (Luke 1:32). Again, this indicated his close relationship to the Davidic Contract promises. In her response (Luke 1:54–55), Miryam expressed gratitude to God for helping his servant Israel in keeping with his promises to Abraham. She understood the Messiah's unique relationship to the Abrahamic Covenant as its source of blessing. Zecharyah (Zechariah), the father of Yochanan the Immerser (John the Baptizer), continues the theme by referring to Yeshua as the Savior from David's house and the fulfillment of promises to Abraham (Luke 1:68–79). And, in a magnificent way, the book of Hebrews highlights Yeshua as the Mosaic Contract's fulfillment and the Renewed Contract's mediator.

An important consideration, deriving from this discussion of the covenants becomes increasingly apparent. Yeshua's death and resurrection have been an important part of God's plan for the ages from the very outset. As Rav Shaul describes it, God planned this "before the creation of the universe"

(Eph. 1:4). As Shimon put it in his prayer: "what your power and plan had already determined beforehand should happen" (Acts 4:28). Furthermore, Yeshua reminded his followers: "I lay down my life—in order to take it up again! No one takes it away from me; on the contrary, I lay it down of my own free will" (John 10:17–18). In other words, the ultimate answer to the question "Who killed Yeshua?" is, in a very real sense, God did! It was his plan from before creation. God's grand purpose had unfolded on the stage of history. The time was finally ripe, and as the ancient rabbi Shaul wrote, God "invaded" planet earth in the person of Yeshua (cp. Gal. 4:4).

Both the Older and Newer Testaments, therefore, make the significance of the covenants quite clear. By studying the Abrahamic Contract, and the Mosaic, Davidic, and Renewed Contracts' elaboration of it, we get a picture of God's plan for his world, Yeshua's central role in God's purposes, and Israel's place in that program. Some of God's promises to Israel have been fulfilled. Others await a future fulfillment as he continues to work with his people through history. It would be a true distortion of the plan of God to miss the centrality of the Jewish people in it, from Abraham through Yeshua, and beyond, into the Messianic Age. The Jews were chosen to bring blessing to the world.

✡   ✡   ✡

Chapter 8

Have the Jewish People Responded to God's Plan?

Frequently when the story is told, the impression the "listener" is left with is that Yeshua's own people rejected him. But, is that really what the Scriptures teach? Is that really what happened?

What Do the Gospels Say?

For example, Mattityahu repeatedly mentions that large crowds of Jews routinely followed him (Matt. 4:25; 7:28; 8:1; 13:2; 14:13; 15:30). These crowds listened to him eagerly and held him in great respect (Mark 12:37). Many of the people believed in him (John 7:31). They even wanted to make him their messianic king! (John 6:15) And, when the leadership hierarchy wanted to arrest him, they hesitated; they realized his following was so large that they would unleash a great riot by making a move against him (Matt. 26:5). In fact, their earlier assessment was: "The whole [Jewish] world has decided to follow him!" (John 12:19).

Their enthusiastic reception of Yeshua climaxed during his "Palm Sunday" entry into Jerusalem to celebrate Passover. The Gospels tell the story (Matt. 21:6–9). As he approached Jerusalem riding on the donkey—a wonderful and well-known messianic picture of that day—"great crowds" lined the streets to welcome him. They cut down palm branches and laid them down on the road before him. The Jewish crowds enthusiastically shouted to him: "Hosanna to the Son of David! Blessed is he who comes in the name of the Lord!" Although the story is familiar, its significance is often lost.

In the late Second Temple period, it was common throughout the Near East to welcome visiting dignitaries by spreading palm branches along the path before them. It corresponded to "rolling out the red carpet." The use of the palm branches had further ramifications. During the wonderful festival of Sukkot, palm branches would be ceremonially waved at special times during the celebration. This was a symbolic way of recognizing God as king and welcoming his presence at the festival. Sukkot was a holiday full of messianic anticipation and images. (For a more complete discussion, see Fischer, *The Meaning and Importance of the Jewish Holidays.*) Recognizing the messianic imagery of Yeshua's entrance, and responding eagerly to it, the Jewish crowds used this custom and warmly welcomed their messianic king.

When they welcomed him with their shouts of "Hosanna," they were doing more than cheering his arrival. "Hosanna" derives from the Hebrew *hosha na*, which means "save us now!" Sukkot was noted for its *Hoshanot* or hosanna prayers. In fact, at the climax of the festival, these hosanna prayers were ceremonially addressed to "the Branch of David," one of prophets' ways of describing the coming Messiah. The crowds used this same phrase, which was full of messianic implications, when they addressed Yeshua.

Significantly, they addressed him as "Son of David." During this time, "Son of David" was one of the most common titles used of the Messiah. It referred to the grand promises God made to David in the Davidic Covenant, mentioned earlier, which included God's promise that the Messiah would come from David's line. By calling him "Son of David," the Jews recognized that David's messianic heir had come.

The crowds also welcomed Yeshua with a common, but significant, Jewish greeting: *"Baruch haba b'shem Adonai!"* ("Blessed is he who comes in the name of the Lord!") The greeting comes from Psalm 118:26. As they celebrated their three most joyful holidays (Passover, Shavuot, and Sukkot), Jews would recite this beautiful Psalm. It is a Psalm that has stirring messianic overtones. Recognizing this, the ancient rabbis suggested it as an appropriate way to greet the Messiah. They would say: "If you live to see the Messiah, greet him in this way: '*Baruch haba b'shem Adonai!*' ('Blessed is he who comes in the name of the Lord!')" Heeding the rabbis' instructions, the crowds welcomed Yeshua as their Messiah in just this fashion.

So, the Gospels make the story very clear. When Yeshua arrived in Jerusalem, the Jewish crowds, in multiple ways, enthusiastically and wholeheartedly welcomed Yeshua as their Messiah.

But didn't these same crowds turn on him several days later and cry "Crucify him!"? As noted earlier—definitely not! That scene took place, as mentioned, on the "Pavement" (Gabbatha) outside Pilate's residence in the Antonio Tower. Its dimensions allow for somewhat just over one hundred people to squeeze into the area, a tiny fraction of Jerusalem's quarter of a million people at Passover time! Moreover, this event takes place during the morning of the preparation for Passover. Few, if any, Jews would have "just happened" to have been wandering around in Pilate's "unclean" neighborhood on that particular morning. They would have been busily preparing for Passover, and making sure they did nothing to ceremonially defile themselves, which would have prevented them from observing the holiday. Pilate's part of town is the very last place they would have entered. This means that those who stood in front of Pilate had been specifically told or asked to be there by the religious hierarchy; they were not the "common people." Additionally, John's gospel indicates that only the chief priests and their Saduccean officials were present before Pilate (cp. 19:6, 15).

So where were the welcoming crowds? What did they do? Luke answers those questions. When they discovered Yeshua was being led away to his execution, the Jewish crowds lined the streets of Jerusalem and cried bitterly because he had been taken from them (Luke 23:27, 48).

Frequently, John 1:11 is cited as evidence that the Jews rejected Yeshua. "He came to his own, and his own did not receive him," the text says. However, the entire earlier context

(John 1:1–10) of that verse speaks of Yeshua's role as the Word with respect to the world as a whole. He created the universe at the beginning. He was the source of life and light for all mankind. He stepped into history and entered his world in order to restore it and reclaim it for himself. But the world he made refused him (John 1:10). Yochanan says the world rejected him, *not* the Jewish people. They received him and followed him in large numbers throughout his life (John 7:31; 12:19).

Furthermore, it was not just the "ordinary people" who warmly accepted Yeshua as their Messiah. A significant number of Jewish leaders did so as well. Torah teachers and experts (Pharisees and Scribes) became his disciples (Matt. 8:19). Synagogue leaders recognized him as Messiah (Matt. 9:18). In fact, "many of the leaders believed in him" (John 12:42).

What About Acts and the Letters?

This ready acceptance of Yeshua not only continued after his death and resurrection, it increased rapidly. At Shavuot, after Shimon preached the important sermon about Yeshua's resurrection, over three thousand more Jews recognized him as their Messiah (Acts 2:41). These numbers grew to well over five thousand a few weeks later (Acts 4:4). And, these numbers soon included "many priests" (Acts 6:7) and important Jewish leaders such as Nicodemus (John 3:1,10), Menahem (Manean, Acts 13:1), and Theophilus (Luke 1:1), all of whom are well known in Jewish literature and history.

By the time Rav Shaul returned to Jerusalem to celebrate Shavuot, Yeshua's brother, Ya'akov, pointed out that thousands of Torah-observant Jews in Jerusalem followed Yeshua (Acts 21:20). The term that Ya'akov used here literally means multiple tens of thousands. Since Jerusalem's estimated population at that time was approximately seventy thousand, it appears that half the Jews of Jerusalem recognized Yeshua as their Messiah!

As for those who did not accept Yeshua, Rav Shaul stands as an enduring example of God's response to those who do not believe: "I formerly rejected him, but I received mercy because I had acted ignorantly in unbelief" (1 Tim. 1:13–14).

What About the Post-Apostolic Period?

It should be noted that, as Augustus Neander—a man often recognized as the "father of church history"—estimated, there were probably over one million Jews who were followers of Yeshua in Israel alone by the end of the first century.

These early Messianic Jews, or Nazarenes as they were often called, did not just fade away. Epiphanius noted in the fourth century that they were still active in the broader Jewish community (*Panarion* XXX, 6:7–9; 18 XXXIX, 7). In the beginning of the fifth century, Jerome remarked that they were found throughout the synagogues of the eastern Roman Empire (*Letter to Augustine*). And, the archaeological remains at Capernaum indicate that they were a viable and vital part of the Jewish community there in the seventh century. Though subsequent centuries submerged the Messianic Jewish movement, due in large part to the violent rise of Islam, Messianic Judaism visibly re-emerged at the end of the nineteenth century in Europe. It vigorously entered the American scene—and shortly thereafter, the international scene—during the latter half of the twentieth century.

What About Today?

Now, there are hundreds of Messianic synagogues in the United States and around the world, comprised of Jews and Gentiles. They model themselves on the practices of the first-century followers of Yeshua, who met in synagogues. These modern Messianic Jews have formed several unique organizations, most notably the Union of Messianic Jewish Congregations (www.umjc.org) and the International Alliance of Messianic Congregations and Synagogues (www.iamcs.org), which is affiliated with the Messianic Jewish Alliance of America. There is also the International Messianic Jewish Alliance (www.imja.com), which operates in some two dozen countries worldwide.

Bringing it back to where it all began, there are approximately thirty Messianic synagogues in the land of Israel. This proves that, despite the misrepresentations of the past 2000 years, there has been a very positive relationship between Yeshua and the Jewish people. And, with a concerted effort, as the next chapter suggests, it will get even stronger.

Once again, as it was for the first half dozen centuries, Jews in large numbers are following Yeshua their Messiah. It is all part of God's master plan for the ages.

✡   ✡   ✡

For Further Reading

Fischer, John. *The Olive Tree Connection*. InterVarsity Press.

Friedman, David. *They Loved the Torah*. Messianic Jewish Publishers.

Leckey, Linda. *The Separation of Early Christianity and Judaism*, unpublished doctoral project. St. Petersburg Theological Seminary.

Pritz, Ray. *Nazarene Jewish Christianity*. Magnes Press.

Schiffman, Michael. *The Return of the Remnant*. Messianic Jewish Publishers.

Schonfield, Hugh. *The History of Jewish Christianity*. Duckworth.

Skarsaune, Oskar. *In the Shadow of the Temple*. InterVarsity Press.

Chapter 9

Does It Matter?

The Fallout from the Passion Plays

Does it matter whether the Passion Plays of the past gave accurate accounts of Yeshua's death? The answer to this question is vitally important, as European Protestants and Catholics realized after the atrocities of World War II came to light. The answer to this question is a resounding "Yes!" Why?

- Because it was the Passion Plays that helped to instill an antipathy toward Jewish people within European Christianity since the 1200s.
- Because it was the Christian Church that created organized persecution of the Jewish people during the Crusades and the Inquisition, killing and exiling thousands of Jews in Europe.
- Because Jewish people were killed by the millions in Europe during the Second World War, and one of the chief reasons given by Nazis for this slaughter was that "They killed the Son of God." A sign hanging over the entrance to one death camp read, "You are here because you killed our God."

Christians do not like to hear that Christian theology was twisted to become a driving force behind Nazism, but it is important for Christians to admit that this was done. American Christians need to understand that just because the Holocaust didn't happen here, that doesn't mean that Christians in America can act as if they are completely without fault.

Each Christian denomination in America claims to be part of the worldwide "family of God," a part of a universal relationship with people from every nation from around the world. Christians cannot just take the "good" and inspiring aspects of being a worldwide community—they have to take the bad parts, too. One of the most shameful chapters in Christian history was the period from 1925 to 1945, in Europe. Unfortunately, churches usually don't teach their laypeople anything about Christian history.

What happened in these European countries that proudly called themselves Christian nations? Jewish communities were destroyed, Jewish businesses were taken over, and Jewish people were forced out of their home countries because they were "Christ killers." Christians took over their homes and businesses, and Christians ran the death camps. It needs to be remembered that in Jewish minds it wasn't Buddhists or Hindus who were in charge; it was Christians. Is it any wonder that many in the Jewish community in America shudder when they hear America called a "Christian nation"?

A Christian seminary professor we know, a fine man of God, visited Israel. He asked his tour guide, an Israeli Jew, "When I say the word 'Christian,' what comes to your mind?" "Three things," the guide said, "the Crusades, the Inquisition, and Nazi Germany." "In that case," the professor replied, "don't call me a Christian."

The God of Abraham, Isaac, and Jacob makes it clear in the book of Genesis that those who bless the Jewish people will be blessed, and those that curse them shall be cursed (Gen. 12:1–3). If American churches truly believe that, then they need to start making up for lost time, because Christianity does not have a history of blessing the Jewish people. Indeed, the vast Christian population did not speak up when the persecution of the Jewish people took place throughout European history. They didn't speak up during the Crusades, they didn't speak up during the Inquisition, and they didn't speak up during the Holocaust. They remained silent, and after the war was over, many Christians claimed that they were powerless to do anything in the face of such an evil Nazi regime. It could be said that Christian silence aided and abetted the Nazis in their "final solution."

Sometimes, evangelical Christians point to heroic Christians like Corrie Ten Boom to prove that there were Christians that loved Jewish people and who suffered in order to save them. Unfortunately, many American Christians have the impression that people like the Ten Boom family lived on every street, which is far from the truth. When asked about any Christian help that they found in the city of Budapest, Hungary during 1944, George and Marianne Fischer (see dedication page of this book) agreed that apart from a local priest who was willing to provide forged documents to Jews to "prove" they were Catholic, there were no Christians available to help them in any way. However, they said, you *might* be able to "buy" a Christian's help.

In fact, there were so few Christians throughout Europe willing to help keep Jews alive that the Israeli government has documented every single one and planted trees in their memory at Yad Vashem, the Israeli Holocaust memorial in Jerusalem. Relatively few trees have been planted along "The Avenue of the Righteous Gentiles"—they number only about 300. If you visit Yad Vashem, you will see the trees labeled for Corrie Ten Boom and her father, along with the trees for Oskar Schindler, Count Wallenburg, and others who were brave enough to risk their lives. As to the argument that the times were so bad that there wasn't anything an "average person" could do, we respond that God uses average people to defy governments and perform miracles, if they make the attempt. Churches are eager to preach that they serve a "miracle working" God, but when miracles were really needed—when Jews were being rounded up and sent to the death camps—where did most Christians go? Back to their homes, to keep safe! Is this what they believe God really wanted them to do? Is this what American Christians will do if times get difficult in America? Is there nothing Americans can learn from European history?

Real Thoughts Lead to Real Deeds

Today, Christians need to realize that it *does* matter what attitudes they teach about Jews and Judaism in their churches—it's not just theoretical, hypothetical knowledge. Wrong and hateful attitudes toward the Jewish people that have been taught in churches have resulted in the death of men, women, and children who committed no other "crime" but that of being Jewish. The "blood curse" in the Passion Plays was used as an excuse for all manner of cruelty against Jews "because they asked for it." Because of this kind of false teaching in the church, Christians were able to look away when Jewish people were being persecuted because of the underlying conviction that "the Jews deserve it."

It matters that Christians explain matters clearly when describing the crucifixion of Yeshua. Yeshua forgave those who tortured and killed him. He asked God to forgive them—and God did! God did not curse the Jewish people into a life of wandering—they were forced into lives of wandering because they bear the name of the God of Israel and suffer for his sake, as their Messiah did.

It matters very much that Christians understand this, because if Christians think that the Jewish people are, in *any* way, still under a curse from God, Christians will think that Jews are deserving of the bad things that evil people do to them. Then, Christians will fail to speak up or act on behalf of Jewish people when persecution comes. They will remain silent and afraid. This is the pattern that took place in Europe as countries fell to the Nazis—it must never happen again. Churches need to actively practice blessing the Jewish people, not just with words and good intentions, but also with deeds.

It matters very much that Christians teach correct theology to adults and children in their churches. Children get their first impressions about Jewish people from Sunday School lessons, especially if they live in an area with few, or any, Jews. What we teach our children may hinder them from forming healthy relationships with Jewish children that they might come in contact with. Generations of Christian children in Europe, who performed in or watched Passion Plays, saw and heard the crowds of "Jews" in the productions call down a curse on themselves. And yet, many of the Christians did not remember the forgiveness Yeshua had for that same small crowd as he was dying.

Today, aspects of Jewish faith and practice may bear little resemblance to those of Yeshua's time. Statements Yeshua made about his Jewish contemporaries should not be indiscriminately applied to the Jewish community today. Note that that Paul identified himself as a Pharisee, and many believe that Yeshua could be considered one as well. We should see Pharisees as the "good guys" in the Passion story—they were against the Sadducees, *not* the apostles.

Why the Film Version of *The Passion* Matters

It matters that Mel Gibson patterned his film around the visions of Spanish and German nuns. Throughout the movie, he portrays the Jewish people as one, unified, angry mob, with an unreasonable and obsessive hatred for Yeshua. Romans are presented as either as psychopaths (most of the Roman soldiers) or as civilized men stymied by the Jewish mobs (Pilate and his right-hand man, Abenader).

It matters that he shows Satan behind the Jewish crowds as the symbolic cause of their actions. He does not show Satan behind the Roman soldiers. It matters that he shows Jewish children with skullcaps tormenting Judas, without explanation. Is this scene supposed to represent reality or merely Judas' vision? The audience is not sure.

It matters that Gibson shows scenes that advance the common Jewish stereotype that Jews love only money. These scenes are not supported by the gospel accounts. It can be said that along with the "blood libel," throughout the ages, Jews have also been smeared with the "money libel"—namely, all Jews are rich, and that they crave money and power above all else. This portrayal of Jewish people was common in Germany and Eastern Europe during the 1800s, and later in the German Weimar Republic and Czarist Russia. This atmosphere produced the lies found in *The Protocols of the Elders of Zion* (see chapter 3). After the First World War, during the Weimar Republic, Jews were portrayed as "Bolsheviks," evil Communist schemers who started the war so they could profit from it. The proliferation of this "money libel" contributed to Hitler's rise to power—he appealed to peoples' fears by championing himself as the leader in the fight against the Bolshevik Jews.

It matters that, in a scene with no explanation for the audience, Gibson portrays an event that *never* happened. He shows the Holy-of-Holies, in the Temple, being physically destroyed at the time of Yeshua's death. This portrays a less-than-symbolic end to the Jewish faith. He shows the Mercy Seat of God as broken. The room that houses it is empty and barren. He presents the rooms of Pilate as more beautiful and appealing than Herod's Temple. This is far from historical truth, and again, misleads people as to what actually happened.

It matters because Mel Gibson set out to present the "gospel" truth in his movie. On the contrary, he made a film that presents a biased version of the story, one with an anti-Jewish spin. It matters because millions of people now and in the future will formulate their perceptions of what happened during Yeshua's last week based on this film and its images, where the suffering is more important than the resurrection, and the dripping blood more important than Yeshua's forgiveness of and love for his people.

It matters in the 21st century because, since September 11, 2001, extremist Muslim groups have identified America as an enemy nation, and labeled us "Zionists and Crusaders." This title identifies America as a Jewish and Christian nation. In the Muslim world, Zionists and Crusaders are invaders of Muslim countries and indiscriminate murderers of innocent Muslims in their homes. Under the labels of primary potency, "Zionists and Crusaders," they have classified all American men, women, and children as their blood enemies, deserving of death. Due to its worldwide distribution, the film is being seen by entire Muslim populations who know little or nothing about the true story of Yeshua's life, death, and resurrection. This is cause for great concern.

It matters in the 21ˢᵗ century because anti-Semitism is again on the rise in Europe, as a report produced in 2003 by the United Nation reveals ("EU Anti-racism Body Publishes Antisemitism Reports"). European nations that have welcomed Muslim residents into their midst have seen fundamentalist Muslim persecution of Jewish people, as has happened in the recent past. In April, 2004, Elie Weisel, an Auschwitz survivor and Nobel laureate spoke to a fifty-five nation conference in Germany where foreign ministers from Europe and North America met to discuss troubling anti-Jewish violence during the last five years. His warning should serve as a chilling reminder to us:

> The Jew I am belongs to a traumatized generation. We have antennas. Better yet, we are antennas. If we tell you that the signals we receive are disturbing, that we are alarmed . . . people had better listen. (qtd. in Moulson 1)

Chapter 10

What You Can Do to End the Distortion

Nearly everyone would agree that the Holocaust was one of the worst—if not the worst—attacks on humanity in all of human history. 6,000,000 Jews, one-third of the Jews alive at that time, were cruelly exterminated by the Nazis.

Incomprehensible as it may sound to us today, this black mark on mankind took place in Christian Europe under the eyes of the Catholic, Lutheran, and other Churches, and was known to the rest of the Western world. Not that all individual Christians participated in the deaths of Jews, but the Church, at large, was silent while Jews were being hung, burned, and shot to death. After World War II, several organizations formed for the purpose of looking into how this disaster happened, and learning how to prevent it from taking place again.

The Insights of Seelisberg

In 1947, an International Emergency Conference of Christians and Jews met in Seelisberg, Switzerland to issue ten significant points aimed at rectifying anti-Jewish elements in Christian teaching. After almost sixty years, they still have not been adopted in many places. The ten points of Seelisberg are shared here as a guide to Christian faith and practice:

1. Remember that One God speaks to us all through the Old and the New Testaments.
2. Remember that Jesus was born of a Jewish mother of the seed of David and the people of Israel, and that His everlasting love and forgiveness embraces His own people and the whole world.

3. Remember that the first disciples, the apostles and the first martyrs were Jews.

4. Remember that the fundamental commandment of Christianity, to love God and one's neighbour, proclaimed already in the Old Testament and confirmed by Jesus, is binding upon both Christians and Jews in all human relationships, without any exception.

5. Avoid distorting or misrepresenting biblical or post-biblical Judaism with the object of extolling Christianity.

6. Avoid using the word Jews in the exclusive sense of the enemies of Jesus, and the words "the enemies of Jesus" to designate the whole Jewish people.

7. Avoid presenting the Passion in such a way as to bring the odium of the killing of Jesus upon all Jews or upon Jews alone. It was only a section of the Jews in Jerusalem who demanded the death of Jesus, and the Christian message has always been that it was the sins of mankind which were exemplified by those Jews and the sins in which all men share that brought Christ to the Cross.

8. Avoid referring to the scriptural curses, or the cry of a raging mob [sic]: "His blood be upon us and our children," without remembering that this cry should not count against the infinitely more weighty words of our Lord: "Father forgive them for they know not what they do."

9. Avoid promoting the superstitious notion that the Jewish people are reprobate, accursed, reserved for a destiny of suffering.

10. Avoid speaking of the Jews as if the first members of the Church had not been Jews.

It seems fairly apparent from this list, compiled only two years after the conclusion of the Second World War, that there were Christians committed to seeing that a Holocaust would not happen again; that anti-Semitism would begin to subside wherever it was found; and that all followers of Yeshua would develop a more accurate understanding of what the Bible really said about the Jewish people and their relationship with him.

These were some serious steps aimed at dealing with the distortion. Now we offer some additional ideas.

Ten More Ways to Overcome the Distortion

We know many Christians who love Jewish people and abhor anti-Semitism. Yet, the mistakes of 2000 years can not rectified overnight. Even so, steps can be taken to foster better relations between Jews and Christians. Therefore, we offer some practical suggestions to set the record straight. We invite you to consider the ideas we provide here:

1. Write down what you thought about Jewish people in general—before reading this book. Has this book changed your thinking on any matters? If so, which ones, and how?

2. Write down what you thought about the relationship between Yeshua and the Jewish people, based on your understanding of the New Testament—before reading this book. Has this book challenged your thinking on any matters? If so, which ones, and how?

3. Ask a Holocaust survivor to come to a group you belong to (church, fellowship, Bible study) to discuss his/her life. Ask them what their opinion of Christians was during the war, as compared to now, to see if their opinions have changed, and why. Ask them what they appreciate most about America. Ask them to give your group their advice about how to survive during difficult times.

4. Set aside time to pray daily for the peace of Jerusalem (Ps. 122:6) and the Jewish people.

5. Learn more about the Jewish community in your own neighborhood to see if there are some projects you or your group could work on together with them (community food bank, voters' registration drives, etc.).

6. The next time you hear someone say something inaccurate about the Jewish people at your job, your

church, or around town, speak up (in a nice way, of course)—don't remain silent.

7. Check out your children's Sunday School materials to see what kind of portrait they are being shown of Jewish people. If your church has a confirmation class of 12–13 year-olds, see if you can arrange for the class to meet together with a local synagogue's Bar/Bat Mitzvah class, or exchange visits as a sort of "Local Ambassadors" project. Have the students compare what they're learning.

8. If you have never been to a synagogue service—go! Check it out. Most likely, you'll be received warmly. Ask about the kind of programs the synagogue offers to its members. Be friendly, and you'll make friends in return.

9. Read books that will help you understand the Jewish roots of your faith. Messianic Jewish Resources Intl. has many such books. For a free catalog of books and other products, call 1-800-410-7367 or visit them on the web at http://www.messianicjewish.net.

10. Attend a Messianic congregation so you can experience, first-hand, how Jews and Gentiles can worship together in a Jewish way.

The impact of the distortion has been vast and subtle. Even the most well-meaning Christian may not understand the positive relationship Yeshua has with his people. Even the most dedicated believer may still think that the Jewish people have, in some sense, been replaced as the chosen people. Vast numbers of churchgoers are convinced that Israel relinquished its God-given right to the land given to Abraham, Isaac, and Jacob when the majority of Jewish people rejected Yeshua. These misconceptions are due, in large measure, to the distortion.

Although damage has been done because of the distortion, God has prevailed. Millions of Jewish people have a positive relationship with Yeshua the Messiah, and tens of millions of Christians do have a clear understanding and appreciation of this unique relationship as well. Moreover, millions of Christians also love Israel and affirm that it is the homeland for the Jewish people.

Yet, much more needs to be done to combat anti-Semitism, correct theological error, and restore relationships between Yeshua and his own people. We hope you will join us as we seek to set the record straight and end the distortion that has existed for 2000 years—that Jewish people and their Messiah don't really have a positive relationship. The fact is—they did, they do, and, in the future, even more will!

Bibliography

Abou El-Magd, Nadia. "Gibson's 'The Passion' a Hit Among Arabs." *Associated Press*, Cairo, Egypt, 5 April 2004.

Albright, William F. "Interview with William F. Albright." *Christianity Today* (January 1963):17–19.

———. *Recent Discoveries in Bible Lands*. New York: Funk and Wagnalls, 1955.

———. *The Archaeology of Palestine*. Baltimore: Penguin, 1960

Aquinas, Thomas. "Letter to the Duchess of Brabant." *De Regimine Principum*.

Beliefnet Staff. "'The Passion': What's Not In The Bible?" *Beliefnet*, 25 February 2004. <http://www.beliefnet.com/story/140/story_14097_1.html> (20 May 2004).

Belloc, Hillaire. *The Jews*. Boston: Houghton Mifflin Company, 1937.

Berman, Daphna. "Jews and Christians are Viewing Entirely Different Movies." *HaAretz*. 3 March 2004. <http://www.haaretzdaily.com/hasen/objects/pages/PrintArticleEn.jhyml?itemNo=401433> (22 April 2004).

Bivin, David. "Jesus' Education." *Jerusalem Perspective* 2 (December 1988): 1–2.

Bock, Darrell. "Jesus vs. the Sanhedrin." *Christianity Today* (April 6, 1998): 47–50.

Bowman, John. *The Gospel of Mark: The New Christian Jewish Passover Haggadah*. Leiden: E.J. Brill, 1965.

Brown, Raymond. *The Death of the Messiah*. New York: Bantam Books, 1999.

Bruce, F.F. *Jesus and Christian Origins Outside the New Testament*. Grand Rapids: Eerdmans, 1974.

———. *The New Testament Documents: Are they Reliable?* Chicago: InterVarsity Press, 1971.

Calvin, John. *Corpus Reformatorum* .Vol. 25, 35, 40, 41, 50.

Carrington, Phillip. *The Primitive Christian Calendar: A Study in the Making of the Marcan Gospel.* Cambridge: Cambridge UP, 1952.

Carroll, John, and Green, Joel. *The Death of Jesus in Early Christianity.* Peabody, Massachusetts: Hendrickson, 1995.

Chattaway, Peter. "Lethal Suffering." *Christianity Today* (March 2004): 36–37.

Cheney, Johnston, and Ellison, Stanley. *The Greatest Story.* Portland, Oregon: Multnomah, 1994.

Dawidowicz, Lucy. *The War against the Jews.* New York: Bantam Books, 1976.

Delitzsch, Franz. *Allgemeine Evangelisch-Lutherische Kirchenzeitung.* (1896).

Drury, James. *Tradition and Design in Luke's Gospel.* London: Daston, Longman, and Todd, 1987.

Emmerich, Anne Catherine. *The Dolorous Passion and Death of our Lord Jesus Christ.* Public Domain: 1823. <http://my.homewithgod.com/israel/acemmerich1/> (13 April 2004).

"EU Anti-racism Body Publishes Antisemitism Reports." *European Union @ United Nations.* 31 March 2004. <http://europa-eu-un.org/article.asp?id=3341> (21 May 2004).

Feldman, Louis. "Is the New Testament Antisemitic?" *Moment* (December 1990): 50–52.

Fischer, John, ed. *The Enduring Paradox.* Baltimore: Messianic Jewish Publishers, 2000.

———. "Foundations of Messianic Theology: In the Footsteps of Jesus." *Mishkan* 11 (1995): 65–89.

———. *The Gospels through Jewish Eyes.* Forthcoming.

———. *The Meaning and Importance of the Jewish Holidays.* Palm Harbor: Menorah Ministries, 1979.

———. *The Olive Tree Connection.* Downer's Grove, Illinois: InterVarsity Press, 1983.

Fischer, Patrice. *The Language Situation in Israel During the Second Temple Period.* Unpublished master's thesis. University of South Florida. Tampa, Florida, December 1992.

———. *The Quest for Jewish Survival in America Since 1967 and the Evangelical Community.* Unpublished master's thesis. Trinity Evangelical Divinity School. Deerfield, Illinois. June 1976.

Flannery, Edward. *The Anguish of the Jews.* New York: Paulist Press, 1985.

Foster, Arnold, and Epstein, Benjamin. *The New Anti-Semitism.* New York: McGraw Hill, 1974.

Fujita, N. S. *A Crack in the Jar: What Jewish Documents Tell Us about the New Testament.* New York: Paulist Press, 1986.

Gerlash, Wolfgang and Barnett, Victoria. *And the Witnesses Were Silent: The Confessing Church and the Persecution of the Jews.* Lincoln: University of Nebraska Press, 2000.

Goldhagen, Daniel. *Hitler's Willing Executioners.* New York: Alfred A. Knopf, 1996.

Gottschalk, Louis. *Understanding History: A Primer of Historical Method.* New York: Knopf, 1950.

Goulder, Michael. *Midrash and Lection in Matthew.* London: S.P.C.K., 1974.

———. *The Evangelists' Calendar: A Lectionary Explanation of the Development of Scripture.* London: S.P.C.K., 1978.

Greenleaf, Simon. *The Testimony of the Evangelists as Examined by the Laws of Evidence.* Grand Rapids: Baker Books, 1965.

Guilding, Aileen. *The Fourth Gospel and Jewish Worship.* Oxford: Oxford UP, 1960.

Hajos, Mary. *Removing the Stones.* Ft. Washington, Pennsylvania: Christian Literature Crusade, 1984.

International Council of Christians and Jews. "International Conference of Christians and Jews. Seelisberg, Switzerland, 1947. *An Address to the Churches.*" <http://www.iccj.org/en/?id=102> (1 June 2004).

"'Jews Killed Jesus' Sign Causing Controversy!" The DenverChannel.com (ABC News). 25 February 2004. http://www.thedenverchannel.com/print/2873395/detail.html> (19 May 2004)

Judge, Edward H. *Easter in Kishiniv: Anatomy of a Pogrom.* New York: New York UP, 1992.

Kistemacher, Simon. *The Gospels in Current Study.* Grand Rapids: Baker Books, 1986.

Lachs, Samuel Tobias. *A Rabbinic Commentary on the New Testament.* Hoboken, New Jersey: KTAV, 1987.

Luther, Martin. *Concerning the Jews and Their Lies. Luther's Works.* Vol. 47.

Meier, John. *A Marginal Jew: Rethinking the Historical Jesus.* New York: Doubleday, 1991.

Mork, Gordon R. "'Wicked Jews" and 'Suffering Christians' in the Oberammergau Passion Play." *Representations of Jews through the Ages.* Eds. Greenspoon, Leonard Jay, and Le Beau, Bryan F. Omaha: Creighton UP, 1996.

Morris, Leon. *Studies in the Fourth Gospel.* Grand Rapids: Eerdmans, 1969.

Morse, Arthur. *While Six Million Died.* New York: Hart, 1968.

Moulson,Geir. "Nobel Laureate Warns on Anti-Semitism." *Seattle Post Intelligencer.* 28 April 2004. <http:// seattlepi.nwsource.com/ap.asp?category=1103&slug =Europe%20Anti%20Semitism> (28 April 2004).

Murphy-O'Connor, Jerome. "Fishers of Men." *Bible Review* (June 1999): 23–27, 48–49.

O'Hara, Robert C. *Language and Meaning.* Dubuque: Kendall/Hunt, 1993.

Ong, Walter. *Orality and Literacy.* London: Routledge, 1988.

Parkes, James. *Antisemitism.* Chicago: Quadrangle Books, 1969.

"'Passion' Stirs Couple to Battle." *St. Petersburg (Florida) Times,* 19 March, 2004.

Phayer, Michael. *The Catholic Church and the Holocaust, 1930-1965.* Bloomington, Indiana: University Press, 2000.

"Poll Finds Passion Strongly Sways Religious Perceptions." *St. Petersburg (Florida) Times,* 11 April, 2004, 7A.

Ramsay, Sir William M. *The Bearing of Recent Discovery on the Trustworthiness of the New Testament.* London: Hodder and Stoughton, 1915.

Robinson, John A.T. *Redating the New Testament.* Philadelphia: Westminster Press, 1976.

———. *The Priority of John.* Oak Park, Illinois: Meyer Stone Books, 1985.

Roth, Wolfgang. *Hebrew Gospel.* Oak Park, Illinois: Meyer Stone Books, 1988.

Sanders, Chauncey. *Introduction to Research in English Literary History.* New York: Macmillan, 1952.

Schneider, Peter. *Sweeter than Honey*. London: Student Christian Movement Press, 1966.

Schwartz-Bart, Andre. *The Last of the Just*. New York: Atheneum, 1960.

Selznik, Gertrude, and Steinberg, Stephen. *The Tenacity of Prejudice*. New York: Harper and Row, 1971.

Shapiro, James. *Oberammergau and the Troubling Story of the World's Most Famous Passion Play*. New York: Vintage Books, 2001.

Snoek, Johann. *The Grey Book*. New York: Humanities Press, 1970.

Sticca, Sandra. *The Latin Passion Play: Its Origins and Development*. Albany: State University of New York Press, 1970.

"Survey Says Number of Americans Blaming Jews for Jesus' Death Rising." *St. Petersburg (Florida) Times*, 3 April, 2004, North Pinellas section, 9.

Thiede, Carsten Peter, and D'Ancona, Mark. *Eyewitness to Jesus: Amazing New Manuscript Evidence about the Origins of the Gospels*. New York: Doubleday, 1996.

Wallechinsky, Richard, and Wallace, Richard. *People's Almanac #2*. New York: Bantam Books, 1978.

Wein, Berel. "Who Knows Bible Best?" *Jerusalem Post* (December 7, 2001): 31.

Wenham, John. *Redating Matthew, Mark and Luke*. Downers Grove, Illinois: InterVarsity Press, 1992.

Whiston, William, trans. *The New Complete Works of Josephus*. Grand Rapids: Kregel, 1999.

Wyman, David. *The Abandonment of the Jews*. New York: Pantheon Books, 1984.

Acknowledgements

We would like to gratefully acknowledge Janet Chaiet for her remarkable diligence in editing this book very quickly and professionally into its final form. And, we wish to thank Barry Rubin for his insight and insistence that made this book a reality.

\# 7015671339 543 1435

Phone (411)

amazone . Com

888 280 4331

1-206 922 0883

---

2 Door bells

1-877 586 3230